ALCOHOL WORDLORE AND FOLKLORE

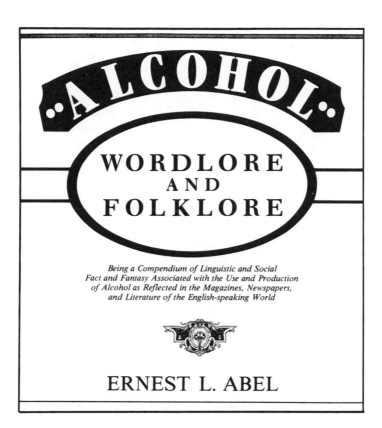

·ALCOHOL·

WORDLORE AND FOLKLORE

*Being a Compendium of Linguistic and Social
Fact and Fantasy Associated with the Use and Production
of Alcohol as Reflected in the Magazines, Newspapers,
and Literature of the English-speaking World*

ERNEST L. ABEL

PROMETHEUS BOOKS
700 East Amherst Street, Buffalo, New York 14215

91 90 89 88 87   4 3 2 1

Library of Congress Cataloging-in-Publication-Data

Abel, Ernest L., 1943-
    Alcohol wordlore and folklore.

    Bibliography: p.
    1. English language—Terms and phrases. 2. English language—Etymology—Dictionaries. 3. Drinking customs—Terminology. 4. Alcoholic beverages—Terminology. 5. Drinking customs. 6. Drinking of alcoholic beverages—Folklore. I. Title.
PE 1683.A24 1987   422'.03   86-30301
ISBN 0-87975-371-4

Introduction

Articles and books about the English language are enjoying greater popularity than ever. H. L. Mencken's *American Language* (1919) has been reissued in paperback, and Stuart Berg Flexner's *I Hear America Talking* (1976) and *Listening to America* (1982) are still on bookstore shelves. John Ciardi's *A Browser's Dictionary* (1983) and his regular commentaries on national public radio, Robert Claiborne's *Our Marvelous Native Tongue* (1983), Paul Dickson's *Words* (1982), William Espy's *An Almanac of Words at Play* (1975), *O Thou Improper, Thou Uncommon Noun* (1978), and *Say It My Way* (1980), and William Sherk's *500 Years of New Words* (1983) are but a few examples reflecting the continued interest in wordlore. And in some circles, William Safire is probably better known for his weekly *New York Times* column "On Language" than for any of his other writings.

There seems to be an insatiable appetite for wordlore, but in most cases wordlore books lack any theme. They are mainly hodge-podges of interesting, oftentimes fascinating, cultural histories of select words having little or nothing in common. This wordlore book differs from others in being unified by the subject of alcohol— its uses and abuses.

Drinking alcoholic beverages is probably as old as fire and the wheel, if not older. From the first accidental discovery of the effects of fermented fruits and grains, man has had a need to describe the sensations peculiar to drinking a little or a lot of the seductive fluids. For evidence the reader should consult Dickson's book *Words,* in which the author cites 2,231 English words and phrases for "drunk," a list consuming 45 of the book's 366 pages!

Drinking has always occupied a central place in English, European, and American life.

Before the nineteenth century, no European or American drank water as an ordinary beverage. England had its ale, Holland its beer, France, Spain, and Italy their wines, and America its ale, cider, and rum.

In America, people drank when they got up in the morning, at meals, when they sealed a contract, at parties, weddings, funerals, when they bought something, when they sold something, at ordinations, at public meetings, when they came, when they went, as a medicinal aid, and before they turned down the covers to go to bed. Or as a sixteenth century Latin epigram so aptly put it, there are *five* reasons for drinking: "Good wine, a friend, or being dry,/Or lest we should be by and by,/Or any other reason why."

Everyone drank. Teetotalism was nonexistent. Every tradesman or laborer expected and received an alcoholic beverage during his workday. Quakers drank. Puritans drank. Clergymen drank. The only restraint was drunkenness. People could drink as much as they wanted; they just weren't permitted to be seen drunk.

Since drinking was so integral a part of life in England and America, pubs, inns, taverns, alehouses, ordinaires, saloons, bars, and the like sprang up to meet the demand and the social custom. At every cross-road and in every community in America there was somewhere to get a drink. These were the gathering places where men socialized and discussed the events of the day.

Since everyone drank and drinking was so much a part of life, it is not surprising that vocabularies were constantly expanding to accommodate the names of different drinks, their physical effects, the cures for treating them, the places where they were sold, the containers they were dispensed in, the entertainments that accompanied them, the brawls that sometimes interrupted them, the efforts to avoid the taxes governments levied on them, the people who tried to change community drinking habits, the laws they passed to enforce their wills, and the numerous ways these laws were evaded.

Not surprisingly, many everyday activities were often described in terms of drinking and its aftermath. People have always found new uses for old words, relating their literal meaning to broader circumstances, attaching what linguists call "extended meanings" and making metaphors of them. It is natural to relate the world to ourselves. Sometimes we make metaphors of parts of our bodies, like the mouth of a river, the foot of a hill, a helping hand, a hard heart.

Although metaphors are appreciated when they first appear, centuries later these same words often continue to be spoken without any awareness of their origins. This is especially so in the case of alcohol. From *butler* to *stockbroker,* from *barmy* to *muggy,* this alcoholic heritage is everywhere. And while their modern meaning is often understood in context, how they came to mean what they do remains an enigma. So, for *befuddled* readers about to take a *swig* of *the whole shebang,* I *pledge* to *distill* the history of these and a *bumper* crop of other words and expressions known to English and American lexicons. I *toast* your approbation and hope that this little book proves to be an *eye-opener.*

Abstemious

"Lead us not into temptation," intones the Lord's Prayer. Good advice. But how do we avoid temptation?

One way is to stay away from anything that might cause us to lose self-control. "Abstinence is as easy for me," admitted Samuel Johnson, "as temperance would be difficult." A thousand years earlier St. Augustine likewise confessed that "total abstinence is easier for me than perfect moderation."

Both Johnson and St. Augustine knew how hard it is to eat just one peanut. That single peanut somehow sets in motion an irresistible urge to have another and another until the whole bowlful is consumed.

The same inability to stop at one or two drinks is why an alcoholic is an alcoholic—he can't stop drinking once that first drop passes his lips. For decades no one ever challenged this presumption. In the 1970s, however, it became one of the most controversial issues in the field of alcoholism. Did the alcoholic have to forgo drinking forever, or could he return to moderate or "controlled drinking"?

To Alcoholics Anonymous (AA), which continues to preach that there is no such thing as moderation for the alcoholic, such an idea was heresy. Researchers in the field of alcoholism such as Drs. Mark and Linda Sobell disagreed. This prominent husband and wife team working with alcoholics had discovered that moderate drinking, as opposed to abstinence, was a viable option for some alcoholics. When they reported their findings, however, they were accused of misinterpreting the evidence. The argument became so heated that it gained national attention in the United States and was featured as a segment of the CBS television program "60 Minutes." The controversy is still unsettled and has generated a bitter battle in which charges of academic fraud have been hurled at the Sobells.

Interestingly, the word *abstemious* has not been used in these arguments, although of all the words used to describe "controlled" drinking, abstemious is the most appropriate.

Abstemious means the same as moderate, temperate, sparing, or not self-indulgent. Unlike these synonyms, abstemious's etymological origins go back thousands of years when it was specifically used to describe the effects of overindulging in alcohol.

Abstemious comes from Latin *abstemius,* the roots of which are *ab,* "away," and *temum,* "strong drink," with its cognates *temetum,* "any intoxicating drink," and *temulentus,* "drunk." Abstemious literally means "away from intoxicating drink," or "away from drunkenness."

Long before it passed into Latin, however, abstemious had its beginnings in the Sanskrit word *tam,*" "to choke," or "to become breathless," which evolved into the Latin *temum.* In India strong liquor was to be avoided because it would make the drinker stop breathing. When the word entered Latin it retained the idea of a drink so potent it could endanger one's health. Instead of *temum,* the Romans drank *vinum,* although they drank it in such great amounts that they might as well have called it *temum.*

Today, abstemious is rarely used to refer to someone's drinking habits. Instead, those who drink abstemiously are called "social drinkers." In his *Devil's Dictionary* (1911) Ambrose Bierce gives abstemious an ironical twist when he defines *feast* as "a religious celebration usually signalized by gluttony and drunkenness, frequently in honor of some holy person distinguished for abstemiousness."

Abstemious is often confused with *abstain* and its cognate, *abstinence*. The latter comes from Latin *abstinere,* "to refrain," the roots of which are *ab,* "away from" and *tinere,* "to hold." From Latin it evolved into the French *abstinir* and then to our present English word.

The difference between abstain and abstemious is one of degree. Abstain means to refrain completely; abstemious means to be temperate in use. Most people probably regard abstainers as morally stronger than those who are abstemious. Not so Ambrose Bierce. To Bierce, an abstainer is "a weak person who yields to the temptation of denying himself a pleasure."

Abstain is actually the older of the two words in English, having entered the language around the fourteenth century; abstemious does not appear until about the sixteenth century. Because of the similarity of the two words, abstemious has lost its special sense of drinking in moderation and now generally refers to habitual moderation in the satisfaction of one's wants and desires, while abstinence means to deny oneself them.

Two other words often used synonymously for abstemiousness and abstinence are *temperance* and *sobriety.* Temperance implies abstemiousness but is often used as a synonym for abstinence, as in the Women's Christian *Temperance* Union (WCTU), an organization completely disallowing alcohol on its premises. *Sobriety* suggests self-control in drinking but has also come to be used as a synonym for abstinence, "sober as a judge" being the epitome of abstinence from alcohol.

Alcohol, alcoholism, alcoholic, workaholic

Cleopatra, who bewitched both Julius Caesar and Mark Antony, used a substance—unknown to Roman women—which the Arabs subsequently called *al-kohl.* *Al* in Arabic simply means "the"; *kohl* means "powder" or "essence." In Cleopatra's day, women heated antimony sulphate until it vaporized, then let it cool so that it would condense. Then they applied the powdery black residue or essence to their eyelids as modern Western women do with eye shadow. Egyptian women to this day emphasize their dark eyes with the traditional kohl.

Centuries later Arab chemists discovered that other substances could be heated and cooled to concentrated forms, and they also called such substances *kohl,* i.e., "essence." When their European colleagues discovered the secret of concentrating the alcohol in wine, they too used the Arab term. Much later temperance writers thought they had discovered a truer etymology for alcohol. They traced it to Arabic *al-qhul,* meaning "evil spirit," which was more aptly suited to their ideas about alcohol. Etymologists remained unconvinced.

The discovery of alcohol came in the wake of alchemy which had begun to flourish in Europe during the thirteenth century. Among the most persistent preoccupations of the alchemists was the search for the "spirit" or elixir of life. In the fourteenth century one such alchemist, Arnold of Villanova, became the first European to isolate alcohol from wine. A native of Spain, Arnold had probably learned the secret of distillation from the Moors.

Until Arnold's time no European had ever consumed any beverage with an alcoholic content higher than 12 percent, because the yeast cells that cause fermentation cannot survive in alcohol concentrations above that amount. The alcoholic content of wine is therefore self-limiting. Distillation made possible beverages with considerably higher alcoholic content, like gin, scotch, and whiskey. To Arnold it was just another step in the search for essences, merely a new application for the centuries-old process of making eyelid coloring.

Arnold may not have appreciated the eventual uses of his discovery, but he liked what he had made and wrote a book about it, calling the distillate *aqua vitae,* the "water of life." "Limpid and well-flavored red or white wine," he said, "is to be digested twenty days in a closed vessel, by heat, and then to be distilled in a sand bath with a very gentle fire. The true water of life will come over in precious drops, which, being rectified by three or four successive distillations will afford the wonderful quintessence of wine. We call it *aqua vitae,* and this name is remarkably suitable, since it is really a water of immortality. It prolongs life, clears away ill-humors, revives the heart, and maintains youth."

Aqua vitae was not a specific name but a general term conferred by Arnold on this magical potion instead of the Arabic *al-kohl.* Arnold's prize pupil, Raymond Lully, liked the term *aqua vitae* but also called it *aqua ardens,* "strong waters." It soon acquired other names like *aqua vitae ardens,* "strong water of life," *aqua vini,* "water of wine," *spiritus vini,* "spirit of wine," and *vinum ardens,* "strong wine." In Germany, alchemists called it *brandewin* "burnt wine," because it seemed so to them. From their word we get our word *brandy.*

The first person to call this distillate *alcohol* was the Swiss alchemist, Paracelsus. Familiar with the Arab process of distilling antimony sulphate, Paracelsus simply applied the Arabic term to this distillate as well, since it was the "essence" or "spirit" of wine.

The English alchemist Francis Bacon (sixteenth-seventeenth century) did not like such generalities, and he retained the term *alcohol* for eye shadow: the "Turkes have a Black powder . . . made of a mineral called Alcohole; which with a fine long Pencil they lay under their eyelids" (*Sylva,* 739). Yet alcohol's roots as an eyelid coloring are now long forgotten except in American slang—and there perhaps accidentally—where liquor is sometimes called "eyewash."

Preventing *alcohol* from assuming a life of its own were its roots in alchemy which saw it as an "essence" of something—the "alcohol of wine." Writers—Coleridge, for example—toyed with expressions such as the "alcohol of egotism." Thus *alcohol* did not come to be used in its present sense until the 1800s.

It was not simply the general tendency for shortening words and expressions that led to alcohol's standing on its own, but developments in the new science of chemistry. When chemists found that the alcohol made from wine was chemically similar to the alcohol in wood and other materials, they looked for a name to apply to this group of compounds resembling one another. They chose alcohol, the name of the first-discovered of these compounds. Each member of the group of alcohols was then given a specific name. To the chemist, the intoxicant we call alcohol is *ethyl alcohol* or *ethanol.* The common chemical structure for all alcohols is carbon (C) joined to a hydroxyl group (OH). The formula for ethyl alcohol is C_2H_5OH.

Alcoholism also made its appearance in the 1800s. It was coined in 1849 by the Swedish physician Magnus Huss to refer to the inability of some people to control their drinking. It took another fifty years for *alcoholic* to make the transition from an adjective describing a kind of liquid to a term for those afflicted by the compulsion to consume it. The noun was omitted from the *Oxford English Dictionary* but was included in the Supplement to OED which cites 1891 as the year of its entry into English. Previously the word used to describe the compulsive drinker was *alcoholist.*

Other words derived form alcohol include *alcoholomania,* alcoholism; *alcoholophilia,* love of alcohol, and its opposite, *alcoholphobia,* fear of alcohol; *alcoholize,* to make into alcohol; *alcoholometer,* an instrument for measuring the alcohol content in a liquid; *alcohology,* the study of diseases caused by alcohol; *alcoholemia,* alcohol in the blood; and *alcoholuria,* alcohol in the urine.

In 1971 author Wayne Oates borrowed the *holic* in alcoholic and added it to *work,* creating a new term, *workaholic.* A workaholic is someone as compulsively attached to work as the alcoholic is to alcohol. "In a very real way," Oates wrote in *Confessions of a Workaholic,* "this land of ours must have workaholics in order to survive as a culture." Since then *-holic* has taken on a life of its own and is attached to any repetitive and seemingly compulsive habit. Now we have *foodaholic, sweetaholic, golfaholic, spendaholic, hashaholic,* and *cokaholic.* Nor have you, dear reader, escaped such a label, for you have been dubbed *wordaholic* by *The New York Times Magazine*: "Only by tracking bromides can wordaholics impose any kind of constraints and make our excellent lingo vogueword free" (23 May 1978, 23).

Ale. *See* **All beer and skittles; Bridal gown, bridal invitation, bridal party;** *and* **Cakes and ale.**

Alembicated

A word that isn't seen or heard very much these days is *alembicated.* From the following context can you guess its meaning?:

"The reading [of Verdi's Requiem] was the alembication of a lifetime's thought and experience" (*New York Times* review, 24 May 1951, 9.3).

Can't tell yet? How about this description of Samuel Johnson's mind?: "like a warm climate, which brings every thing to perfection suddenly and vigorously, not like the alembicated product of artificial fire" (Mrs. Piozzi, *Anecdotes of Samuel Johnson,* 1786, 197).

If you haven't yet guessed, alembicated means "very concentrated, very refined, sublime." It comes directly from the world of distillation through *alembic,* the cap or beak of a still.

Still is the shortened term for distilling apparatus. The three basic parts of a still are the boiler, also called the kettle or cooker, in which the raw material is heated; the alembic, also called the cap or beak, which sits on top of the boiler gathering the vapors and directing them to the condenser; and the condenser, also called the worm, which cools the vapors and in so doing transforms them back into liquid.

Since different substances have different boiling points, they vaporize at different temperatures and therefore can be separated. Alcohol vaporizes at 78 degrees centigrade; water, at 100. By keeping the heat of a mixture of alcohol and water above 78 but below 100 degrees, alcohol can be separated from water.

Strickly speaking, *alembic* refers to only one part of the still, but it very early came to be used as a general term for the whole unit. Arabic in origin (from *al,* "the," and *inbiq,* "still"), the first recorded use of the word in English dates to Chaucer in 1374. Several hundred years later in 1790 it was finally freed from its literal shackles, when, in his description of the French Revolution, Edmund Burke spoke of "the hot spirit drawn out of the alembic of hell."

Variants of alembic such as *limbeck, lambyke, lembike, lembyck,* and *lembeck* were used figuratively much earlier. The *Oxford English Dictionary* cites yet another spelling of the word found in a sixteenth century love poem in which the still is a metaphor for the writer's ardor: "My love doth serve for fire, my heart the furnace. . . . The Limbique is mine eye that doth distill the same."

All beer and skittles

"Life isn't *all beer and skittles*" is a once-common expression, which originated in the English pub. Figuratively, it means life is not all pleasure; it is not just drinking and playing. In true British understatement, Kipling used the expression to describe a soldier's first encounter with the rigors of army life. Soon after the recruits "fell in for their march," says Kipling, "they began to realize that a soldier's life was not all beer and skittles" (*The Drums Fore and Aft,* 1899).

Beer, a beverage containing between 3 and 6 percent alcohol, is made by fermenting barley or other grains with hops. This is in contrast to *ale* which is made without hops. Nevertheless, in earlier days the Anglo-Saxons used the term *beer* (or rather its Old English counterpart *beor*) for their ale, a dark, sweet, alcoholic beverage made with malt, yeast, and water—then the most common drink in England. *Beor* fell into disuse until the fifteenth century when it was revived and applied to the popular European beverage introduced to England by the Flemings (Germanic people inhabiting what is now northern Belgium), in order to distinguish it from ale.

At first the English were appalled at the bitter taste of the upstart import and refused to drink it. As a result, the price of beer plunged so low that Henry V gave it away to his troops while they were besieging Rouen. In so doing he saved about half what it would have cost had he supplied them with ale. By 1419, however, beer had gained a foothold on English soil, and beer brewers were distinguished from ale brewers.

Still there were opponents. Some, like Andrew Boorde (*A Dyetary of Helth*) warned:

> And nowe of ate dayes it [beer] is much used in Englande to the detryment of many Englysshe men; specyally it kylleth them the which be troubled with the colycke, and the stone, and the strangulation; for the drynke is a cold drynke; yet it doth make a man fat, and doth inflate the bely.

During the eighteenth century, a dark-brown variety called "entire beer" was sold; it later became known as "porter," presumably because of its popularity among that group of laborers. Dickens himself may have preferred it, since instead of "beer and skittles," he wrote: "It's a regular holiday to them—all porter and skittles" (*Pickwick,* ch. 41).

Skittles was a game similar to bowling except that it was played on a lawn with nine pins, and instead of a ball, a flat disc was thrown at the pins to knock them down. It was played in the American colonies until outlawed by Connecticut Blue Laws. To circumvent the law the colonists added a pin and called their game ten pins. This new game became the modern antecedent of the present American pastime, tenpin bowling. Skittles is still played in Europe, but in America it is found only in the form of skittleball, a type of bowling game for children in which a ball attached to an elastic is hurled at pins. (*See also* Brew, bread, broth, *and* Porterhouse.)

Amethyst

Long before "diamonds were a girl's best friend," many women, married women especially, cherished the amethyst over all other precious stones.

The amethyst is a six-sided variety of quartz whose purple or bluish-violet color is due to impurities such as iron or manganese. Although a beautiful stone, the amethyst's value in ancient times rested not in its beauty or rarity but in its magic.

The source of the alleged power of the amethyst is seen in its derivation from the Greek *a*, meaning "not," and *methuein,* "to be drunken," which in turn stems from Greek *methu,* "an intoxicating drink." (During the early part of this century, the Presbyterian Temperance Board of Pittsburgh, Pennsylvania, recognizing the etymology of the word, named their anti-drinking monthly magazine *Amethyst.*) The root goes back even further to the Indo-European *medhu,* "honey" which gave rise to *mel* in Latin and *medhu* in Sanskrit. The latter are related to the English word "mead," a wine made from honey.

As reflected in its derivation, the Greeks believed that the amethyst would protect them against drunkenness. For this reason they used to put it in the bottom of their drinking cups. Those who could afford to embedded amethysts in the sides of their goblets.

The belief about amethyst's magical properties originated in a myth concerning Bacchus, the Greek god of wine. According to the myth, the usually playful Bacchus became irate one day because of an insult by another god. Since he could not avenge himself on another deity, Bacchus decided to take out his anger on a mortal, declaring that the first person he encountered on earth would be attacked and eaten by a tiger. The luckless person happened to be a beautiful young girl named Amethyst on her way to worship at the goddess Diana's shrine. As the tiger lunged toward her she called out for Diana's help. To prevent Amethyst from being mauled and devoured, the goddess turned her into a white stone. When Bacchus saw the transformation, he felt remorse for his cruelty and poured grape juice over the stone as a sign of his regret. The white stone then took on its present violet color. The Greeks believed that just as the maiden was saved from the god of wine, her stone would protect them from Bacchus as well.

Because of their alleged magical power to prevent drunkenness, amethyst amulets were very popular among women. Women have always worried when their husbands have gotten drunk, for a drunken husband has often beaten his wife or children or caused chaos in a household. Indeed, as Beer's Calendar for 1825 describes him: "A drunkard is the annoyance of modesty; the trouble of civility; the spoil of wealth; the distraction of reason; he is only the brewer's agent; the tavern and ale-house benefactor; the begger's companion; the constable's trouble; he is his wife's woe; his children's sorrow; his neighbour's scoff; his own shame; in summer, he is a tub of swill; a spirit of sleep; a picture of a beast, and a monster of a man." To ward off the evils of drunkenness, women hoped that the amethyst amulets worn around their necks would protect them by keeping their husbands sober. Even though experience proved the superstition wrong on countless occasions, the myth that the amethyst could protect a drinker against drunkenness survived into the Middle Ages.

By analogy, the amethyst's power to prevent intoxication caused by wine was extended during the Middle Ages to the intoxication of love. Lovers who feared becoming overly passionate kept their ardor in check by wearing amulets of amethyst (spelled *amatist*—the "lover's stone"—from Latin *amor*).

Scientists are now trying to find drugs with amethyst-like properties and have coined a new word for such agents—"amethystics." Describing research in this area being conducted at the University of California at Irvine by Dr. Ernest Noble, the former director of the National Institute on Alcoholism and Alcohol Abuse, *Newsweek* magazine announced that one day a sobering-up pill might be available (1 November 1976, 63). According to the report,

> subjects [in Dr. Noble's experiment] . . . tossed off 6 ounces of gin
> or vodka. They were next given either a moderate dose of one of the
> three drugs [aminophylline, ephedrine, or L-dopa]—or a placebo,
> and their relative degree of inebriation was measured. Alcoholic
> impairment of the critical ability to process information was reduced
> by as much as 50 per cent in those who had taken the drugs, known
> as *amethystic* agents.

The amethyst is also highly regarded as the birthstone for February. Belief in birthstones—special stones believed to confer special characteristics on those born during a particular month—first became popular in Poland, largely through the influence of the Jews who settled here. Exodus 28:15-30 contains a detailed description of the jewels in the breastplate to be worn by the High Priest Aaron and specifies that the amethyst is to be set with the agate and jacinth in the third of four rows of gems. The significance of the twelve breastpiece gems can be found throughout Talmudic commentaries and in other rabbinical writings. Soon after Polish Jews started wearing birthstones, the fashion spread to other Poles who liked the idea of wearing a stone perceived as both a talisman and a reflection of the wearer's personality.

Although the amethyst is considered February's birthstone, in astrological circles it is the gem most closely associated with Pisces (February 21 to March 21), and there is an old poem about the sobering effect of the amethyst for Pisces' children:

> From passion and from care kept free
> Shall Pisces' children ever be
> Who wear so all the world may see
> The amethyst.

(*See also* Drunkard.)

Appeal from Philip drunk to Philip sober

In business, in sports, in law, in practically every course of life timing is everything. It's not enough to know that something is a good investment, you have to know it's a good investment when the value of its stock is low. You've got to jump into the market at just the right time before everyone else does so as well, thereby raising the price.

In sports, athletes hone their bodies to the very edge so they "peak" as close to the day of the contest as possible. In law courts attorneys have found that through judicious scheduling, a case might be heard by a judge more favorably inclined to their client than if another judge presided. In business, a request for a raise might be successful if the boss is in a good mood, but the same request heard when he's in a bad mood might result in a tirade about "value paid for value received."

When looking for an objective and unbiased judgment about some critical matter, don't ask someone who is excited or distraught. Better to wait until that person is calm and prepared to give your problem serious and dispassionate deliberation. But if your timing is off, you might want to *appeal from Philip drunk to Philip sober.*

The Philip in this expression was King Philip of Macedon (third century B.C.), father of Alexander the Great. Although Philip ruled Macedon with the proverbial iron fist, he had a reputation for fairness. One day when listening to his subjects' grievances Philip was drunk and decided against a woman who sought justice for some wrong. On hearing the king's judgment she immediately cried out, "I appeal." Surprised at the outburst since *he* was the final authority in the land, Philip demanded to know, "To whom do you appeal?" "I appeal," answered the woman, "from Philip drunk to Philip sober." Not too drunk to recognize the sagacity of the comment, Philip agreed to hear the case on another day and subsequently ruled in the woman's favor.

Assay

Anytime precious metals, such as gold or silver, are bought or sold, they must be assayed. An *assay* is a test to establish the presence and quantity of a particular substance.

The most famous assay in history occurred some 2000 years ago. Hiero, the king of the Greek city of Syracuse, had received a crown purportedly made of silver. How much silver he was not sure, nor did he want to melt it down to find out, for that would have meant destroying the crown. But how else could he determine what the crown was really made of? Baffled, he turned to the greatest mind of his time, the famed mathematician, Archimedes.

Archimedes pondered the problem for a long while but couldn't figure out how to do what the king wanted. Even while other problems demanded his attention, Archimedes' mind was unconsciously trying to solve the enigma of the crown.

One day while filling his tub and meditating on the crown, Archimedes put too much water into the bath; when he sat down, water poured over the side onto the floor. Instead of cursing, Archimedes shouted "Eureka!" the Greek word for "I found it!" (Various embellishments of the story have him getting out of his bath and running naked through the streets shouting "Eureka!" to all the town.)

Apocryphal or not, Archimedes did indeed discover an assay method for determining how much precious metal is contained in an object. When Archimedes sent the bath water splashing onto the floor, it occurred to him that his body—and every body—displaces a specific amount of water whenever it is immersed. By placing metals of known purity in water and noting their displacement, he could quantify the presence of like metals in an object without having to melt it down. (Genius favors the prepared mind!)

Throughout the centuries methods of assaying or testing for purity of metals were always being sought. But despite numerous advances in the technology, in life and death situations, there was only one sure method relied on by all kings and nobles—the human assay.

In bygone days one of the chief means of obtaining power or wealth was by killing those who had it and taking over after their death. An easy way of accomplishing this goal was by poisoning someone's food or drink, usually the latter because that was more easily accomplished. To foil any such attempt, many of those in power had servant-"assayers". These servants were often doctors, and their duty was to make certain their master's food and drink contained no poison. In England, the court physician was the chief assayer. Usually both food and drink were assayed twice, each time by different individuals. The most important part of the assayer's job was to taste portions of a meal before it was served to the lord or noble.

The two main beverage assayers were the butler and the cupbearer. In the wine cellar the butler would take the first drink. He would then pour the wine into a large vessel and give it to the cupbearer who covered it and brought it into the dining hall. In the dining hall the cupbearer uncovered the vessel, poured some of the wine into an assay cup and drank it in the presence of the master. These assay cups often contained a charm or a piece of horn, supposedly taken from a unicorn and alleged to neutralize any poison poured into the cup. If the wine had been poisoned, the butler and the cupbearer assayers would die, and the lord would be spared. In some castles an assayer even tasted the water in which the lord and his guests washed their hands before eating. This assay was also performed in front of the principals.

Because poisoning was so common, assayers were placed at the disposal of every guest in wealthy homes. Not to assign an assayer to a guest was a gross sign of disrespect. *Hall's Chronicle,* a sixteenth century work, clearly describes the role of the assayer in the attempted poisoning of King Richard II, together with the King's reaction. According to the historian, when King Richard visited Sir Piers Exton at his castle, Sir Exton, who intended to poison the King,

> forbade the esquire which was accustomed to serve and take the
> assaye beefore Kyng Richarde, to again use that manner of service.
> [Unknowingly, the king] sat downe to dyner, and was served with-
> oute courtesie of assaye; he much mervaylyng at the sodayne mu-
> tacion of the thynge, demanded of the esquire why he did not do his
> duty. The esquire replied that Sir Piers had forbid him to perform
> his duties pertaining to his position. The King immediately picked
> up the carving-knife, struck upon the head of the assayer, and ex-
> claimed "The devil take Henry of Lancaster and thee together."

Assay is actually an alternative form of *essay* which comes to us from the Latin *exagium,* a "weighing," through Old French *essai,* a "trial." The person performing the test was the *essayer. Assai* was a variant of the Old French word. Both versions passed into English, but each assumed a different connotation while still retaining its original sense. Today *essay* is usually a written composition demanded of students to test their writing skills, or an interpretive literary composition, whereas *assay* generally refers to a test for the purity of metals.

Bacchus, bacchante, bacchanal

A recent guide to American universities rates these institutes of higher learning according to a number of parameters, one of which is hedonism. Not all university education goes on in the classroom, but in some universities learning seems to place second, and a distant second at that, to social events. The "toga party" in National Lampoon's movie, *Animal House* (1978), was not too different from the drunken *bacchanals* I witnessed during my university days at a relatively conservative college in Toronto.

The *bacchanal,* whether it occurs in college or elsewhere, has a long history. Originally it had religious overtones associated with Dionysus, the Greek god of wine whom the Romans called Bacchus. In Greek mythology, Dionysus was the son of Zeus and one of Aphrodite's lovers. He combined drunken revelry and sexual abandon. "Bacchus," said poet Thomas Fuller (*Gnomologia,* 1732), "hath drowned more men than Neptune."

In *The Bacchae,* written in the fifth century B.C., Euripides describes how Bacchus first came to Greece. According to the dramatist, Bacchus is very upset with King Pentheus of Thebes because he won't recognize his divinity and prohibits his subjects from worshipping him. Only the women dare secretly to pay homage to Bacchus. They become priestesses or *bacchantes* and furtively go to the hills to engage in mysterious rites. When King Pentheus hears about their clandestine activities, he decides to go there disguised in women's garments to see for himself what is going on. On the way, however, Bacchus makes him insanely drunk and the women mistake him for a wild animal, kill him, and cut off his head. His mother, who is one of the *bacchantes,* believes his head to be that of a lion and takes it back to the palace as a trophy. Bacchus is now satisfied that the insult has been expiated and his divinity is no longer doubted. (During a performance of the *Bacchae* in Parthia in 53 B.C., the head of the Roman general Crassus was substituted for the prop when the time came to carry Pentheus's head to the temple. The grisly sight first shocked the audience, but their shock soon turned to cheers at this dramatic announcement of the Roman army's defeat.)

Whether they called him Dionysus or Bacchus, the *bacchantes* (masculine, *bacchanalians*) celebrated their devotion in ecstatic dancing, singing, sexual abandon, and of course drinking. These rites were well known in Shakespeare's day: "Shall we dance now the Egyptian bacchanals, and celebrate our drink?" (*Antony and Cleopatra,* 2.7.104) and very often the celebrations got so out of hand that the authorities had to be called in to arrest participants for disturbing the peace.

In *The Lips That Touch Liquor,* written in 1870, composer George W. Young used *bacchanal* as a synonym for lasciviousness. The poem and its language, especially that of the last line, appealed to the Temperance Movement which adopted it as one of their standards:

> Your lips, on my own, when they printed "Farewell,"
> Had never been soiled by the beverage of Hell;
> But they come to me now with the bacchanal sign
> And the lips that touch liquor must never touch mine.

Today *bacchanal* has become a plaything of punsters; *New York* magazine's review of a concert called it a "bacchanal with Bach et al" (12 November 1984, 134).

The adjectival form of Dionysus, the Greek name for the god of wine, has also been applied to revelry and sensuous pastimes. Although Russians are not known for Dionysian gambols, their spies have no compunctions against such diversions. The home of Russian spy Guy Burgess, for example, was known as "a center of dionysianism for highly placed people in wartime London" (*New York Times,* 25 January 1976, 7.3). In philosophy, however, the term refers not to carousing but to the Nietzschian view of creative, imaginative activity as opposed to deliberate, sober thinking.

Reviewing the then current Burt Reynolds movie *Hustle,* J. Kroll invited readers to "walk with Burt through the grubby cubicles of the L. A. Police Department as he hears the foot fetish man do his *dithyramb* about smelly ladies' feet" (*Newsweek,* 12 January 1976, 69). Though foot odor is far removed from the bouquet of wine, the god of wine was also known as Dithyramb, and the wild, ecstatic poems, songs and music composed by his votaries in his honor were called Dithyrambic, an eponym still used to describe any poem, song, speech, or diatribe delivered emotionally or passionately like that of the foot fetishist in the movie.

Bacchus also lent his name to several other words usually not thought of as related to inebriety. Although many university students spend a large percentage of their time in *bacchanalian* revelry, most of them eventually receive their *baccalaureates,* or "bachelor of arts." The baccalaureate degree is derived from Bacchus through Latin *baccalaureus,* a "bachelor who has successfully completed the first tier of learning in a university."

Bald-faced

Reacting to an accusation that the Christian Voice, a conservative evangelical group, was distributing report cards on congressmen "as if they were mandated by God or the Bible," president Gary Jarmin denounced this claim as "an absolute bald-faced lie" (*Insight,* 25 August 1986, 23).

A *bald-faced* lie is one so transparent it deceives no one. This American slang term has nothing to do with lack of hair, however. Instead, it refers to unaged whiskey. Bald-faced whiskey was raw and not easily disguised. It was not a beverage for the faint of stomach. There was no way an unscrupulous seller could substitute this inferior product for a better, brand-named whiskey.

The earliest usage of this Americanism was recorded in the 28 April 1840 issue of the *Daily Penant,* a St. Louis newspaper. The expression did not become colloquial until the 1850s, however, and the *New York Knickerbocker Magazine* for November 1848 (xxxii, 402) had to explain to its readers that the drink "classically denominated 'bald face' . . . [was] brown whiskey." Bald-faced soon disappeared as a description of inferior whiskey, but the bald-faced lie is still very much with us.

Balderdash

Cousin to *baloney, blarney, bunk, horsefeathers,* and many other words signifying "nonsense," *balderdash* means ideas or arguments that don't go together. Before it had this connotation, *balderdash* referred to an incongruity involving adulteration or dilution.

In 1637 the self-styled "Water Poet," John Taylor, said that balderdash was a mixture of beer and wine: "Beer, by a mixture of wine hath lost both name and nature, and is called balderdash" (*Drink and Welcome*). Ben Jonson, a contemporary, said it was beer and buttermilk (*New Inn,* 1.2). Thomas Smollett (*Travels.* ch.

14) wrote that "the wine-merchants of Nice brew and balderdash. . . ."

How balderdash came into English is still unsettled. Some etymologists trace it to the Danish words *balder,* "noise," and *dask,* a "dash." The "dash" is understandable, but why call the mixture a "noise"? If you mix beer and wine or beer and buttermilk together you don't get an explosion. On the other hand, during the 1600s, brewers began experimenting with various ways of adulterating their beer in order to increase their profits. Watering down their brews was, of course, an obvious way to cut costs. Adding sugar to speed up fermentation was also commonly done. While such practices are accepted now, in the Middle Ages people expected their beer to be served "neat"—free of any foreign substance. Brewers were heavily fined for trying to cut corners, and customers usually made a lot of noise (*balder*) when they complained.

Balderdash must have been a very popular word in the early 1600s, for it was transferred in the latter part of the century from an incomprehensible mixture of liquids to an incomprehensible mixture of words and ideas. "Balderdash!" was an especially popular retort during the 1890's but has been almost completely replaced by the more earthy "Bullshit!" which came into its own in the 1930s. You can still come across *balderdash,* however, in novels like James Clavell's *Tai Pai:* "Great spheroids of balderdash, how can you think about a doxy's tail when you're in the presence of a master-piece?" or in Canadian newspapers which seem to have a fondness for the word. An editorial in the *Toronto Star* (3 October 1984), for instance, dismissed warnings about Canada's budget deficit as "balderdash." On another occasion, the paper referred to Member of Parliament Betty Stephenson's charges of school elitism in Canada as "balderdash" also. And the *Vancouver Sun* brings the word back full circle, having categorized a local ruling on alcoholism as nothing less than "balderdash" (2 March 1982, A1).

Barmy, balmy

Barmy means "scatter-brained," "empty headed," or "confused." Although occasionally traced to St. Bartholomew, patron saint of the feeble-minded, barmy's origin is more superficial than recondite. When yeast is added to fruits or grains to speed fermentation, the froth or foam that rises to the top after the mixture has fermented is called "barm." "Of windy cider and of barmy beer," wrote Dryden in his translation of Virgil's *Georgics*. In the Roman's day barm was especially prized by women as a facial cleanser, but it was more commonly sold to bakers who used the yeast in barm to leaven bread.

According to the *Oxford English Dictionary,* barmy was first recorded in its original sense in 1535; by 1594 it was beginning to gain figurative meaning. "My wits work like barms, alias yeast, alias sizing, alias rising, alias God's good," wrote Lyly (*Mother Bombie,* 2.1.117). Two antithethical English proverbs eventually developed from this figurative sense, one recognizing innate intelligence: "His brains will work without barm," and one suggesting that drink was needed to encourage intelligence: "His brains will *not* work without barm."

In more modern times *barmy* is used to describe someone whose brain has fermented and become frothy—an "airhead." For emphasis there is the expression, *barmy in the crumpet,* meaning slightly unhinged or "touched in the head."

In England, the *barmy ward* was the area of jail reserved for the criminally insane—the *barmies. To put on the barmy stick* was to feign insanity so that one would be transferred to the *barmy ward.*

Despite their prodigious acting skills, few imposters from the jails ever got away with feigned madness, says Michael Davitt in *Leaves From a Prison Diary.* The difficulty in deceiving the medical staff was that each prisoner was subjected to constant surveillance before any transfer was approved. Keeping up the act for twenty-four hours a day for many weeks at a time was just too much for most imposters. Those whose trickery was uncovered were quickly returned to their former quarters but not before being given a severe flogging.

Davitt, who spent time in Millbank, Dartmoor and Portland prisons in the late 1800s, tells the story of one such *barmy stick* at Dartmoor known as "Barmy Flanagan." Flanagan was a consummate actor whose ruses included writing a letter to his grandmother asking her to request a visit from Queen Victoria so that they could "renew old acquaintance." While the Queen was visiting she could also act as a witness to his will, said Flanigan, who told his granny that he was planning to leave his doctor £5,000 "for the kind treatment he has given me." Such tactics almost fooled his captors into thinking him a genuine lunatic. But Flanagan was done in by a seemingly innocent act—he was found reading the instructions given to the warders for observing his behavior. The doctors felt that curiosity and madness did not mix, and "Barmy Flanigan" was returned to his former cell "deservedly punished and cured."

It was not simply because prisoners were shirkers that they "put on the barmy stick." Prison conditions in England before the turn of the century were deplorable, whereas the insane were treated more humanely. They were not rigidly disciplined, they were assigned less work, and they received better food. Books such as Davitt's, which described these conditions and chronicled the lengths to which prisoners would go to escape them, disturbed the public and played no small part in Lord Kimberley's recommendations for the reformation of the British penal system.

Balmy is a variation of *barmy* and has exactly the same meaning. Dick Swiveller in Dickens's *Old Curiosity Shop* had a preference for the *l* spelling and "balmy sleep." The unknown poet of *Salvation Sally* also preferred the *l*:

> The people in our alley call me Salvation Sally,
> Since I have been converted, but I try to bear the load;
> They say I must be *balmy* to go and join the Army
> That leads to salvation in the Whitechapel Road.

Barrelhouse

Barrelhouse jazz is loud and "hot." It's not the kind of music one is likely to hear in a posh nightclub where the accent is on refinement. Barrelhouse jazz is at home with a clientele interested more in drinking than in listening.

During the late 1800s a barrelhouse was a saloon without much refinement, where barrels of beer were kept in the open along one wall of a narrow room. On the other side was usually a table containing tumblers or mugs. For five cents, a customer could ostensibly stand at any barrel and drink as much as he wished. If he tarried too long, however, he was thrown out. In these days beer was called "barrel goods," alcoholism was called "barrel fever," and alcoholics were called "barrelhouse bums." "As its name implies," wrote Herbert Asbury in his history of New Orleans in the late 1800s, "the barrelhouse was strictly a drinking-place, and no lower guzzle-shop was ever operated in the United States" (*The French Quarter*, 231).

In the late 1890s itinerant musicians began congregating in Storyville, New Orleans' legalized red-light district, playing a new kind of music called "jazz." Too poor to afford real instruments, the musicians improvised on old kettles, cowbells, and gourds filled with pebbles, or used drums, whistles, horns, and bull fiddles made from half barrels. Usually they stood outside the ignoble brothels or saloons (by then also called barrelhouses), playing for passing customers and perfecting their style. Eventually the uniqueness of their music began to be appreciated, and they were invited inside to play. Jelly Roll Morton, Louis Armstrong, and many other jazz greats perfected their artistry in these barrelhouses.

During the next two decades jazz began to flourish and to develop into a distinct American genre. While still very much improvised, it is now more formal and prescribed than during its formative years. During the Prohibition era raucous, improvised barrelhouse music was still played in cheap speakeasies catering to a poor clientele, where music was offered but no one went to listen. These places were often so disreputable that *barrelhouse* came to mean any run-down, shoddy speakeasy, brothel, or lodging house.

Bartender

Bartending is not an easy job. For one thing you have to work nights. There's no point being able to concoct the perfect martini at 8:00 o'clock in the morning. For another, you have to be a good listener. A bartender probably hears as many confessions as some priests but unlike a priest, he can't give absolution—only an occasional "Un huh," or "Yah, I know what you mean."

A bartender must know how to pacify an unruly drunk and not bother the other customers. He has to know when to say no to someone asking for another drink, and if this doesn't work and no bouncer is on the premises, he has to be able to apply the "bum's rush."

Some bartenders work full time; others, one or two nights a week. Some take the job because they need the extra money; others who earn more than enough money work behind a bar simply because they like it. They like to listen as well as to talk about what's happening to baseball, to politics, to the neighborhood.

But for whatever reason they take the job, the most important thing bartenders must know is how to make a drink. Not just one drink, mind you, but at least thirty or forty. They have to know which are served "on the rocks" and which "straight up"; which are stirred, which shaken and which mixed in a blender like a Piña Colada. And they have to know what kind of glass to serve it in—a cocktail, highball, collins, sour or champagne glass.

Like a pharmacist reading a doctor's prescription, a bartender must be able to decipher a waiter's shorthand: "Screw" is a screwdriver (vodka and orange juice served in a highball glass with ice); "7/7" is 7-Up and Seagram's 7 whiskey; G/T is gin and tonic; "WSr-R" is a whiskey sour on the rocks.

A novice bartender will use a "shot" glass—usually a one-ounce glass with a line indicating the half-ounce mark. A good bartender can pour a half-ounce, ounce or ounce-and-a-half drink, with either hand, without a measuring device.

Before there were bartenders, there were bars. The word *bar,* meaning a place where alcoholic drinks are served, occurs as early as the 1600s, but *bartender* wasn't coined until the 1800s. Prior to that time the job was performed by a *barkeeper,* sometimes familiarly known as a "barkeep." Today a bartender is likely to call himself a "mixologist," and bartending in America is no longer an all-male job.

The father of American mixology is Jerry Thomas, affectionately known as the "professor." Thomas worked as a bartender in San Francisco during the middle 1800s at a resort known as the El Dorado. It was during this fledgling period that he first became famous by foiling a holdup with one of his drinks. Drinking legend has it that a gang burst into the El Dorado, brandished its guns, and demanded all the receipts. Thomas kept his cool when lesser men would have trembled, asking calmly whether the bandits wanted a drink before they went about their business. The men seemed in no hurry and sat down to accept Thomas's offer.

So enchanted were the bandits with Thomas's concoctions, with one drink leading to another, that finally the whole gang was lying on the floor in a drunken stupor. In that condition they were easily relieved of their weapons and hanged with great fanfare by the local vigilantes. At the hanging everyone begged Thomas to tell them the recipe that had so "captivated" the holdup men but Thomas refused. He claimed it was nothing special, not very artistic and wouldn't gain him much money if he sold the recipe. He also swore he would never serve it again—unless a similar emergency arose.

From the El Dorado Thomas moved into the California gold fields where he struck gold, taught the local bartenders a little of his alcoholic artistry, and started a minstrel band that toured the area. Although he was a success at each of these endeavors, he one day disappeared. No one knew why or where he had gone until a miner told of having met Thomas and challenged him to make a particular drink. Thomas accepted, but when the miner told him what it was, the bartender had to confess his ignorance. Told by the miner that it was native to Central America, Thomas took off for that part of the world to learn more.

When he returned Thomas became the principal bartender at two of America's most famous restaurants: the Planters House in St. Louis and the Metropolitan Hotel in New York. He was constantly inventing new cocktails and eventually recorded his recipes in a book published in 1862, entitled *How to Mix Drinks or The Bon Vivant's Companion,* whose universality was reflected in its subtitle: *Containing Clear and Reliable Directions for Mixing all the Beverages Used in the United States, Together with the Most Popular British, French, German, Italian, Russian and Spanish Recipes, Embracing Punches, Juleps, Cobblers, etc., etc., etc., in Endless Variety.* So great was the demand for the book that it went through at least six reprintings and served as the bartender's bible of drinks in every fashionable bar in America for almost fifty years.

Although bartending was dominated by males in the United States, in England it was a profession for women, continuing a tradition dating back to the Babylonian Code of Hammurabi (circa 2000 B.C.).

In England in the Middle Ages every household that could afford to brewed its own ale. Those who couldn't afford to, went to ale-houses for their ale. There it was served to them by barmaids called alewives, who brewed the beverage as well.

The alehouse catered primarily to the lower classes and was often a gathering place for disreputable characters. Because of the nature of the clientele, the alewife felt no need to be concerned about either her looks or her brewing methods and very often she tried a few shortcuts, like putting soap in a tankard to give it an artificial head, dishonest practices which got her into trouble with the aleconners appointed by the local government to keep an eye on alewives. Although never accused of such trickery, one such alewife, an Elynour Rummyng who lived in the early 1500's, was described by the poet John Slelton, tutor of King Henry VIII:

> Her face was Lyke a rost pygges eare,
> Brystled wyth here
> and her nose, Never stoppynge,
> But ever droppynge . . .

When more men got into the business of brewing, they organized themselves into a guild which alewives were prevented from joining. This precluded their doing any more brewing, and they had to content themselves with only serving ale or at best owning an alehouse. (*See also* Brewster.)

Bead, raise a bead

During the 1700s and 1800s, a *bead* was an idea and *raising a bead* was a popular expression for ensuring success or bringing something to completion. "That idea of your'n . . . carries a fine bead," says a character in James Fenimore Cooper's *Deerslayer* (ch. 6). This bead had nothing to do with jewelry or the sight of a rifle. Instead it came directly from making whiskey, the bead being the small bubble or bubbles that form on the surface of good liquor. If a batch of liquor did not have the right strength, a bead would not form. If it did, the bead would rise to the top.

Beer. *See* **All beer and skittles** *and* **Brew, bread, broth.**

Befuddled

"You look befuddled," said the voice behind me.

"Huh?"

"I've been watching you from my desk," said the librarian. "You have a befuddled look on your face."

"That's amazing!" I said.

Now it was her turn to look befuddled. "What?"

"That's amazing. Befuddle's the very word I've been looking up in these dictionaries."

The librarian didn't seem to know what I was talking about. She was the essence of befuddlement.

"I've been trying to research the history of *befuddle*," I told her, explaining that I was writing a wordbook about alcohol.

"Oh," she said, the befuddlement now gone from her face. "Have you checked . . .?" and she rattled off the names of a number of historical and etymological dictionaries.

I had checked but hadn't gotten very far. We exchanged more befuddled looks. She excused herself with an offer to help if there were anything else I needed, and I went back to the dictionaries.

Befuddlement seems quite common these days. Inventor Joseph Newman says he has invented a new machine "whose ingenious principle is so simple it befuddles the mind" (*Omni,* December 1985, 20). A few years ago "recession and federal attitudes befuddle [d] the growth [of the pollution control] industry of the 1970s" (*New York Times,* 4 July 1975, F4). During World War II, "Indian Marines befuddle [d] the enemy" by talking in the native tongue, which might as well have been proverbial Greek to the Germans (*American West,* November 1981, 67).

According to the *Oxford English Dictionary* and various etymological dictionaries, *befuddle* seemed to be an orphan, simply popping into our language from nowhere in the 1880s. No roots. No history. OED merely noted its existence and added a comment to see the *be* prefix. No help there. The Supplement to the OED, published many years later, cited a 1930s reference as its earliest appearance. The 1937 edition of *Webster's Universal* lists it without etymology and defines it as "to mystify; to confuse; to muddle, as with drink." And therein lies the clue.

The OED had the answer all along but didn't know it. *Fuddled* is an old slang term for drunk. The OED traces its origin to the sixteenth century. The Brewers' Guide of London in 1702 provided this recipe for making strong ale: "Thames water taken up about Greenwich at Low-water when it is free from all brackishness of the sea and has in it all the Fat and Sullage from this great city of London, makes very strong drink. It will all itself ferment wonderfully and after its due purgations and three times stinking, it will be so strong that several Sea commanders have told me that it has often fuddled their murriners." In 1737 Ben Franklin recorded the word in his *Drinkers Dictionary*. In those days to get drunk was *to fuddle one's cap*, a drunkard was known as a *fuddle-cap*, an ordinary drink was called a *fuddle*, an excellent drink was a *rum fuddle*, and a drinking spree was called being *on a fuddle*.

Befuddled is no orphan.

Binge

There are all kinds of binges: eating binges, spending binges, sleeping binges, sexual binges, and, of course, drinking binges. A *binge* is a prolonged bout of some activity, usually lasting more than a day.

Binge is a word of many facets. In parts of England in the 1500s one meaning of the word was "a bow" or "curtsy"; in other parts of the country, however, it meant "sour." In the British navy, binge meant to soak a cask or barrel with water to remove any alcohol that might have dissolved in the wood. There is also a possibility that binge is a combination of *bung*, the hole in a barrel through which the contents were removed, and *bilge*, the last part of the contents. The current sense of an unrestrained, extended drinking spree seems to have started in, of all places, staid Oxford University in the late 1800s. While *binge* may have been coined in those erudite halls, the idea has been expressed in about a hundred different ways, including the following:

at a booze fest	on a bat
alcoholiday	on a bender
bacchanal	on a blind
bacchanalia	on a blow
bacchation	on a blow out
bouncing	on a Brannigan
buster	on a bun
giving nature a fillup	on a bust
going to town	on a drunk
got his skates on	on a hummer
have a jag on	on a jag
have a time	on a racket
heel kicker-upper	on a rip
hell around	on a randan
hell's a-poppin' loose	on a rantan
hellbender	on a razzee
hey-heyer	on a razzle-dazzle
hi-de-ho	on a rummer
high goer	on a shindy
high jinks	on a shitter
high go	on a skate
hitting it up	on a soak
jagster	on a souse
jingling	on a splash
jollying up	on a spree
joy riding	on a spreester
jubilating	on a tear
kicking up one's heels	on a tipple
kicking up the devil	on a titley

letting 'er go	on a toot
letting 'er go Gallagher	on a twister
letting 'er snort	on a weeping jag
letting 'er tear	on a wing-ding
letting go	on the loose
letting off steam	on the merry-go-round
long stale drunk	on the sauce
making a night of it	riding out of town with
making hell pop loose	nothing but a head
making hey-hey	stale drunk
making things look crimson	tearing up
merry hell	throwing a wind-ding
merrymaking	whooping it up
	whoop-de-do

Bogus

Referring to ongoing talks between Russia and the United States in 1980, *U.S. News & World Report* suggested that while Russia's diplomats talked peace and reconciliation, "her secret agents were busy concocting bogus notes to blacken America's image" (3 March 1980, 68). Anything *bogus* is fraudulent, false, misleading. A bogus $20 bill is counterfeit.

Bogus unquestionably originated in the United States, but its etymology has been hotly debated. One explanation poses an eponymous origin. In the 1830s an Italian mountebank named Borghese became very wealthy passing forged checks throughout the southwestern United States. When Americans coined their word for false money, the contention is that they used Borghese as their source.

Eric Partridge in *Dictionary of the Underworld* rejects this explanation in favor of the more mundane and simple *calibogus*. This was later shortened to *bogus* and referred to a popular American drink made with rum and spruce beer, which to some was as incongruous a mixture as that used in balderdash. *Webster's Universal Dictionary* (1937) claims that the word's origin is uncertain but lists as one of its definitions "a mixture of rum and molasses." The *Century Dictionary* (1900) likewise calls its origin uncertain but adds that it may have followed from *bagasse,* "sugar cane refuse." This also would relate it to the alcoholic beverage, since rum is made from sugar cane. The *Oxford English Dictionary* hedges, giving its origin as bagasse, i.e., rum, or bogus, "a liquor made from rum and molasses."

The earliest documented use of *bogus* occurs in the 6 July 1827 issue of the *Plainesville Telegraph,* an Ohio newspaper, which referred to counterfeiting plates, rather than the money made from them, as bogus: "He never procured the casting of a Bogus at one of our furnaces." Thirty years later *bogus* achieved figurative sense: "Crocodile tears," declared an American minister, "are bogus" (Dow, *Patent Sermons,* 4, 216). Some erstwhile guardians of the American tongue refused to acknowledge its existence, however. Describing a criminal trial taking place in Boston, the *Daily Courier* of 12 June 1857 declared: "The learned judge took occasion to manifest his abhorrence of the use of slang phrases . . . by saying that he did not know the meaning of 'bogus transactions.'" The judge's refusal notwithstanding, the rest of the country thought it was worth adding to the lexicon.

By the 1860's, *bogus* had crossed the Atlantic but was still regarded as a distinctly American term by *Cornhill Magasine:* "A mere juggle, or as Americans would say, a 'bogus' parliament." Several years later, Michael Davitt, whose story of prison life in England has already been mentioned (*see* Barmy), was writing of "the bogus nobleman" as someone who "is always of good address, and shines particularly in conversation, as, I suppose, the real article does when met with in society." Apparently, by Davitt's time *bogus* was a well-known word in Britain. *Bogus* eventually underwent a further and unique development there, coming to mean anything tiresome or dull, as expressed by one of Evelyn Waugh's characters in *Vile Bodies:* "'Oh, dear,' she said, 'this really is all too bogus.'" (*See also* Balderdash.)

Boon companion

A *boon companion* is a "good friend," a "buddy," a "pal." The *boon* or "good" part is a corruption of the French word, *bon.* Before it came to have this general connotation, a boon companion was someone who spent a lot of time in a tavern drinking beer, as this quotation from a play written in 1600 by Thomas Nashe shows: "What a beastly thing is it, to bottle up ale in a man's belly, when a man must set his guts on a gallon pot last, only to purchase the alehouse title of a boone companion?" (*Pleasant Comedy,* 1.1125).

Three hundred years later, the term gained back its original sense when *Newsweek* described CIA operative Edwin P. Wilson as someone whose "affinities for boozing, whoring and telling tall tales won him lots of boon companions" (20 August 1984, 71). Used in this context, the term evokes its original, specific meaning of "drinking buddies," rather than the more general meaning of "good friends."

Bootlegger

The person who makes, transports, or sells illegally made whiskey is a *bootlegger.* The term originated in the United States during the close of the nineteenth century and referred to the illegal sale of alcohol to Indians, a practice antedating the coining of the word by a couple of centuries.

Some of those who broke the law hid their bottles of alcohol in the top of their boots and covered them with their pant legs. Whiskey concealed in this way was called "bootleg," and *bootleg whiskey* became a generic term for illegal whiskey. The *Oxford English Dictionary* quotes an 1890 New York newspaper, the *Voice,* as the first recorded instance of the term. During the Prohibition era *bootleg, bootlegger, and bootlegging,* were among the most common words in America. No one was in any doubt about what the *San Francisco Chronicle* was talking about on 16 February 1924 when it reported: "United States Senator Frank L. Greene of Vermont was shot and seriously wounded while walking on Pennsylvania avenue near the Capitol tonight by a prohibition agent in pursuit of bootleggers."

Soon after its coinage, *bootleg* took on a life of its own, becoming synonymous with "smuggled." In 1928 the *London Observer* (5 February, 18.2) wrote that because of Bostonian censorship "books are bootlegged in Boston as liquor is bootlegged in other cities." The following year *Variety* (19 April, 1.2) was talking about "bootleg disk records."

After Prohibition, *bootleg* lost most of its impact but reappeared in the 1960s. This time it wasn't liquor but cigarettes that were bootlegged. To avoid high cigarette taxes imposed by states in the northeast, cigarette bootleggers (dubbed *buttleggers*) drove large trucks down to North Carolina where the state tax was only two cents a pack and brought cigarettes up to New York and other highly taxed northern states. The buttleggers then sold the cigarettes to merchants at a profit. The merchants in turn sold them at the state-imposed price without reporting the sales and pocketed the difference.

To combat the problem, the tobacco industry formed The Council Against Cigarette Bootlegging which did nothing more than publicize the revenues lost to northern states. These were said to be about $110 million for New York State alone in 1976. A cut in taxes was also proposed, but as *Time* (4 October 1976, 80) noted: "Cutting taxes might well reduce the buttleg traffic, but it would also cost the state an estimated $33 million a year in lost revenue—assuming of course, that the buttleggers do not take over all the business. "

In the 1950s, sports also adopted *bootleg* into its lexicon, where, in football, the term referred to a legal, albeit surreptitious act by the quarterback. Instead of throwing the ball or handing it off to one of his teammates, the quarterback only pretends to do so while actually concealing it as best he can. While the opposition pursues the wrong man, the quarterback runs with the ball until the ruse is discovered and he is brought down or pushed out of bounds. Although this ploy is not illegal, the act of hiding the ball evokes the time when liquor was hidden in the boot.

Booze

Booze is a universal slang term for alcohol. In Arabic the word is *buze;* in Persian, *buza.* Hindustani has *buza;* Turkish, *boza;* and Russian, *busa.* The English form possibly arose from Old Dutch *buyzen* through Old English *bouse.* In each of these cases, the literal meaning is "to drink deeply." In some rural districts of England a *booze* was a cattle trough.

Although the word *booze* has a centuries old past, it did not become a popular term for drinking alcohol until the middle 1800s in the United States. The precipitating event was the emergence of the "Booz" bottle, named after Edmund G. Booz (died 1870), a Philadelphia importer and dealer in wines and liquor. The bottle in which he sold his liquor had a distinctive two-story log cabin design with the date 1840 stamped on the roof and the inscription "E. G. Booz's Old Cabin Whiskey," on the side. The popularity of the log cabin motif was inspired by William Henry Harrison's successful campaign for the presidency, the log cabin being a symbol used to represent Harrison's humble origins.

Bread, brew, broth

From humble beginnings, the origins of which are lost in time, people have brewed beer and raised it to the multibillion dollar business it is today. The oldest recorded example of brewing comes from Egyptian heiroglyphics which depict this ancient vocation.

According to these ancient writings, the art of brewing was born in blood. An Egyptian legend carved in stone during the reign of King Seti I describes how the goddess Hathor came to earth one night so enraged at some offense to her honor that she massacred everyone she encountered. Seeing the streets running with blood, Ra, the chief Egyptian god, sent for fruit and had it mixed with ground barley and the flowing blood. During the night Ra spread the mixture onto the fields where Hathor had been wreaking her terrible vengeance. When the goddess returned in the early morning, she saw her face reflected in the flooded field and her image so appealed to her that she drank the beer, became drunk, and forgot all about her mission of death. Thenceforth to appease her, priestesses regularly offered beer as a sacrifice at Hathor's altars.

In its most specific context, *brew* means to make beer or ale by steeping malt or hops or other materials in water; afterword, the mixture is boiled and then allowed to ferment. Since tea is steeped in water, we also say that tea is brewing. In America *brew* is a synonym for beer.

The etymology of the word is relatively straightforward. It comes from Middle English *brewen* through Old English *breowan,* which in turn comes from Old German *briuwan* through Old Frisan *broute,* and ultimately to Latin *defrutum,* meaning "boiled down" or "fermented." The same Latin root gave rise to our words *broth* (the liquid in which something has been boiled) as well as *bread.* Old descriptions of brewing show that the early stages of preparation for making bread and beer were exactly the same:

When a sufficient quantity of brewer's barm is collected, it is put into thick bags or sacks, a number of which are placed together in a press and squeezed for some time. . . . When the liquor is completely extracted from the bags . . . the residuum is left to dry in the bags under the weight of the press, and only drawn out to be sold to bakers, or such as may require it. One pound of this barm will serve to leaven five hundred pounds of dough for the lightest bread (Morewood, *A History of Inebriating Liquors,* 390).

The similarity between the early phases of brewing ale and baking bread also led to the expression, "As you brew, so shall you bake." This proverb is contained in a song entitled "The Brewer" in Thomas D'Urfey's *Pills to Purge Melancholy* (vol. 3, p. 25) written about 1696, but is undoubtedly older than that. Nathan Bailey included it in his *Divers Proverbs* in the 1700s. Literally, it meant that if the brewing process were not done properly there would be no barm to leaven the bread. Another proverb with similar intent is "As you make your bed, so shall you lie." Both mean that we all are ultimately responsible for our actions. If we do well, we will be rewarded accordingly.

By extension, anything fermenting or concocting, whether in a vat or in someone's mind, is brewing. Figurative use of *brewing* occurs as early as John Dryden's 1672 play, *Amboyna,* Act 1, Scene 1: "Why this now gives encouragement to a certain Plot, which I have been brewing." In further extensions, "storms began brewing in the South," "trouble began brewing" in various parts of the world, and "is still brewing in the Middle East." Even architectural design gets into the act: "Brewing for nearly three decades but only widely known for a few years, these stylistic alternatives to the status quo are now gathered under the rubric of postmodernism" (*United,* June 1984, 61). (*See also* Barmy.)

Brewster, Conners, Malter, and other surnames

Ever since Alex Haley's book *Roots* (1976) became a bestseller and later a popular TV series, people from every walk of life have become excited about finding their own roots. While it is often very hard to trace ancestries through every generation, one of the best clues to ancestral occupations is contained in our own surnames. Although it is impossible to examine every surname here, some of those whose origins lie in the beverage industry can be mentioned.

Open any British or American telephone book and look up the surnames *Brewer, Brewere, Brewster, Broster, Bouwer, Brower,* and *Bruster.* All derive from the ale- and beer-making industries dating to thirteenth century England. Ale was the favorite and predominant drink in England during the Middle Ages until about the fifteenth century when beer was introduced into the country from Europe. Given a choice between ale, beer, or water, virtually no one chose water.

Anyone could make ale in his own home, but to sell it, he had to abide by some very stiff regulations aimed at protecting consumers. During the Middle Ages ale was made by mixing malt, yeast and water. Nothing else could be added. There was no hops whatsoever in medieval ale. After it was made, it could not be sold until it had stood for at least five days.

The making of ale was called *brewing,* and the makers were *brewers.* When people started adopting surnames in the eleventh and twelfth centuries, those who made their living brewing and selling ale adopted or had bestowed upon them a surname reflecting their occupation. The earliest known surname of this sort was that of Richard Briwerra whose name can be found in records dating back to 1192; nine years later Adam the brewer—Adam le Browere—was recorded. The *London Telephone Directory* in 1984 listed 235 Brewers and 139 Brewsters.

People with surnames like *Malster, Maltas, Malter, Malthouse, Malthus,* and *Maltman* are all related to ancestors whose job was making the malt used by brewers to make ale. The name Hugh the Malter—Hugh le Malter—is recorded as early as 1306.

Chuck *Conners* and Mike *Conners* were two well-known TV and movie personalities. They and others with the same surname had an ancestor whose job was to inspect ale produced by brewers.

If it were not up to local standards, the *conner* could fine the brewer or force him to put a lower price on his brew. To detect brewers who were illegally adding sugar (a practice some brewers adopted in the sixteenth century to speed up the brewing process), the conner would pour some of the brewer's ale onto a table; then he would put on leather breeches and sit on the table for a few minutes. If he stuck to the table as he got up, he presumed the ale contained sugar, and the brewer was in for trouble. Another name for this inspector was alefounder, and as early as 1381 the name John Alefoundere was recorded. It is a surname still found in Essex and Suffolk.

Other surnames that spring directly from the alcoholic beverage industry are *Goodale, Goodall, Godhale, Goodhall, Goddayle,* and *Gaudale,* which were bestowed upon brewers whose ales were considered better than most. *Meader, Meder, Medur,* and *Medemaker* are surnames derived from ancestors who made *mead,* a popular wine drink made by fermenting honey (called mead), malt and yeast. Wine did not become really palatable until well into the Middle Ages; nevertheless, it was still an important beverage in Europe dating from the beginning of recorded history. People who made or sold wine were called *vintners,* and from that trade name came the surnames, *Vintner, Vintiner, Vintor, Vyner, Wingard, Winyard,* and *Wynyard.* Those who grew the grapes from which wine was made were named *Vigne, Vignes, Vines, Vinens,* and *Viners,* from the French *vigne,* meaning vine.

Britons whose ancestors were engaged as assayers have such surnames as *Sayer* and *Saer.*

Tapper designates a beer-seller or tavern owner, for the tapper was originally the one who opened or "tapped" (Old English *taepere*) the casks.

Today *tipple* means to drink, and a *tippler* is someone who drinks more than he should. But the family name *Tipler* does not stem from drinking too much; instead it comes from the Middle English, *tipeler,* "a seller of ale."

To insure that customers got the amount of wine or ale they

paid for, there had to be a system of measures. This gave rise to the *Disher* family name, which refers not to dish makers but to artisans whose job was to make wooden measures for wine and ale. (*See also*, Assay *and* Butler.)

Bridal gown, bridal invitation, bridal party

Life was very hard during the Middle Ages, but one respite people had from their daily toils was the popular *ale*. This was the name given in England to social gatherings often sponsored by the Church. At such festivities there would be dining, dancing, and singing, all accompanied by great quantities of ale.

Ales were also put together for special occasions. A *help ale* would be convened to raise money or food for those who had become sick or whose house had caught fire, or who were generally in need. *Give ales* were parties in honor of someone who had died and bequeathed money to the Church for ale to be drunk in his memory.

Another of the popular ales was the wedding party, or *bride's ale,* honoring a bride-to-be. A day or so before the wedding, friends and relatives would give the intended bride supplies and equipment to make ale which the bride would sell and serve at the wedding celebration. These gifts and the money she earned would help the new couple start their new life together.

The word *bride,* meaning a newly married woman, is not related to *bridal* but is Irish and comes from *Brid* or *Bridget,* the goddess of covenants, including marriage. So esteemed in Ireland was Bridget that she was canonized. In Wales, her veneration is reflected in the large number of churches dedicated to St. Bride. Our word *bridal,* however, comes not from the saint but from the custom of the *bride's ale,* later shortened to *bridal.* Another related *ale* shortened to *al* is *betrothal.*

We still have a "bride-ale" party, but we call it a *bridal* party. And it refers not to the post-wedding celebration (reception) but to the immediate families of the bride and groom. Guests invited to the wedding receive *bridal* invitations, bring presents, express their wishes for the couple's future happiness, and frequently comment on how lovely the new bride looks in her *bridal* gown. Although a lot of alcohol is still consumed at weddings, ale is no longer the favored drink, and the bride's only duty is to look radiant and happy.

Broker, brooch, broach, brochure, brocade

One of the better commercials appearing on TV showed a group of people on an airplane, in a sailboat race, or in a social gathering. Everyone is either minding his own business or socializing. The camera then zooms in on two people talking in a low voice about investments. One of them says, "My broker is E. F. Hutton." Immediately everyone arounds them stops talking and leans toward the speaker to hear what the seemingly omniscient broker has had to say.

A broker today is a middleman. He arranges things, usually financial transactions, between buyers and sellers and takes a commission or brokerage fee for his services. If he deals in stocks, he works in a brokery, or brokerage house.

Broker made its appearance in its present guise in the fourteenth century, but it was not until the seventeenth century, when European stock markets came into being, that it was applied to *stockbrokers.* Before that it also referred to buyers and sellers of stolen goods—the modern-day "fence." Even earlier there was the *love-broker*—the person who arranged sex between people—a pimp or panderer. The goal of the *marriage broker* is to forge a more lasting relationship, presumably one based on spiritual rather than sensual love. If the marriage fails, the wife may try to sell her ring to a *pawnbroker.*

Broker comes from Latin *broccator,* the wine merchant who opened, i.e., "broached," the wine cask. In ancient France, Latin *broccator* became *brokiere,* "a broacher," and the *brokiere* became a wine salesman, or middleman between the winemaker and the wine merchant or seller.

From those early beginnings opening wine casks, the broker has carved a position first as a sex agent, then as a mainstay and dominant force in the financial markets of the world, and, finally, as a Power Broker (the title of a book by Robert Caro published in 1974 about a middleman who wielded political power).

Closely related to broker is *brooch,* an ornamental fastener, usually for jewelry such as necklaces or bracelets. Like the broker who serves as a middleman, the brooch performs the same task for inanimate objects.

Broach comes from the same root but is more closely related to Latin *broccus* and Italian *brocca,* a "spike," or "pointed head" and more specifically to the spike used to broach or open casks. When a broker sensed that a business arrangement might be made between two people who otherwise were unaware of one another, he would *broach* the subject to both prospective clients, or open the subject for discussion.

A *brochure* is a pamphlet that opens a topic for the reader. It may be an essay on why we should do something, or it may describe the attractions of a particular place or thing.

Still another word from the same root is *brocade.* Brocade is a fabric with a raised ornamental design made with the *broccus* or "pointed head," which in addition to opening a cask could also be used for stitching.

Bucket shop

For a little city in the heart of America's midwest, Little Rock, Arkansas, has had more than its share of notoriety. In 1957 because the governor of Arkansas defied U. S. desegregation law, President Eisenhower sent troops of the 101st Airborne Division to Little Rock to protect nine black teenagers seeking admission to Little

Rock Central High School. Little Rock was segregation's last stand, and it lost.

Those days are far behind. Little Rock has grown. It has a thriving population of 159,000 and is emerging as America's mortgage capital.

Mortgage capital? Little Rock, Arkansas?

After the state in 1983 passed a law removing a ceiling on interest rates, legitimate and spurious firms moved into Little Rock and started aggressively selling investments by phone to buyers a-round the country. Legitimate companies were welcomed. But as *Newsweek* magazine observed, "Little Rock has more than its share of bucket-shop operators whose slick salesmen make the most of their customers' gullibility" (2 December 1985, 69).

A *bucket shop* is an unauthorized business which buys and sells stocks and operates outside the guidelines established for the stock exchange. Run by dishonest brokers, the bucket shop caters to gullible speculators rather than to investors. Its image lacks respectability.

Originally such shops offered customers shares of stock considerably smaller than could be obtained from regular dealers. There was never any execution or delivery of securities, however, nor any intention of doing so. This was pure speculation, and often these disreputable places simply closed up shop and disappeared after taking their customers' money. Many clients took their losses philosophically, prepared for such an untoward event, as the *New York Evening Post* suggested, by their vocations: "[It is] notorious," declared the newspaper on 24 February 1908 "that bucket shops and wild cat promoters generally find clergyman and college professors their most unresisting prey."

Although these shops operated outside the rules and regulations of the legal exchanges, they used their terms and forms, and the genuine shops began to suffer by the confusion. However, "As curb traders grew richer," explained *Time* magazine, "they got rid of 'bucket shop' brokers and became a respectable proving ground for new securities" (6 January 1947, 82).

Before *bucket shop* was used to describe these gambling exchanges, a bucket shop was a "dive," or saloon that sold beer by the pitcher or literally by the bucket. The *New York Evening Post,* in October 1881, explained how the dishonest stock exchanges were christened: "A 'bucket-shop' in New York is a low 'gin-mill,' or 'distillery,' where small quantities of spirits are dispensed in pitchers and pails (buckets). When the shops for dealing in one-share or five-share lots of stocks were opened, these dispensaries of smaller lots than could be got from regular dealers were at once named 'bucket-shops.'"

Bull pen

If you have ever watched baseball on television or listened to a game on radio, invariably you have had to put up with a break in the action while a manager calls on his bull pen for a relief pitcher. In baseball jargon this means that the present pitcher is being relieved of his job for that game, and another pitcher who has been practicing in a restricted area of the ball park, called the *bull pen,* is being summoned to take over.

Calling the new hurler a "relief" pitcher is understandable, but why call the practice area a bull pen? It's not as though the pitcher were an unpredictable wild animal needing to be confined to protect the other players. So why bull pen?

The *bull* in bull pen has nothing to do with bulls or any other animal. Baseball may have the title of America's "national pastime," but the real national pastime of Americans is drinking, and much drinking occurs in bars. Some patrons become rowdy after having too much to drink, and when this happens they sometimes run into the "bouncer," a burly, tough-looking character whose job is to break up any fights and evict unruly customers.

Today such people will be thrown out onto the street. But during the heydey of saloons an enclosure with a high board fence was located next to one of the rear exits, and into it obstreperous customers were thrown until they sobered up. These enclosures were called bull pens, not because the customers were acting like wild bulls, but because *bulling* meant watering down or diluting liquor.

The term *bull* was originally nautical and appeared in such phrases as *bull the cask,* or *bull the barrel.* It stemmed from the practice of pouring water into an empty rum cask to keep the wood moist. After steeping for some time, the rum in the wood would leech back into the water and would provide a very intoxicating drink. Sea captains tried to deter their men from drinking this grog by using salt water instead of fresh. In this case the grog was called *salt water bull.* Another use of the word *bull* to refer to liquor occurs in the expression *bull-dozed,* meaning very drunk. Putting someone in the bull pen was thus a way of diluting his aroused spirits.

The idea of a pen where someone waited until it was time for his release and the idea of *bulling,* or using something twice, were eventually applied to baseball's practice area where pitchers warm-up, or "brew," until it is their turn to enter the game.

Bumboat

Long before the rumrunners of the American Prohibition era, *bumboats* sailed up and down English rivers and coastal waters.

These were usually very wide vessels that brought fresh food to boats at anchor or ferried captains from the shore to their ships. In addition to such legal activities, these boats were also used to bring liquor to seamen who could not go ashore. During the eighteenth century so much smuggling of liquor and other goods took place on the Thames that Parliament passed the Bumboat Act of 1761 to deal with the problem.

These boats were called bumboats because of their very wide hulls and because they often carried liquor. To many, they resembled the large drinking jugs called *bombards* which were common in England during the sixteenth and seventeenth centuries, in the days when heavy drinkers were called *bombard-men.* In analogy with these oversize ale bottles, the oversize transport vessels filled with liquor were called bumboats.

Another possible explanation for the term stems from the word *bum.* While this has long been slang for buttocks, *bum* also refers to an idler (from German *bummer,* a "loafer") and is slang for a drinking spree: "Thursday night is the favorite time," wrote a chronicler of Yale's student life in the 1870s, "for the more depraved Stones men to go 'off on a bum' together, and afterwards wake the echoes of the college yard with their discordant howlings." (The more things change . . .) In the sixteenth and seventeenth centuries children in England used to call a drunk, a *bum.* Years later in America the same person was called a *drunken bum* or *stew bum.* By extension, the boat that brought alcohol to waiting seamen may have earned its name from the effect of its illicit cargo.

Bumper

In the midst of famine in countries like Ethiopia, other lands are blessed with fertile and productive farmlands. Many are more than able to feed their own people and to sell or give tons of grain to less fortunate nations. Even though these countries outproduce most countries on an annual basis, every now and then we hear that farmers have produced a bumper crop of soybeans, or wheat, or corn, meaning that they have greatly exceeded expected production. Ironically, these large harvests often become economic liabilities, as noted by the *Christian Science Monitor:* "Europe's bumper crops may add to Common Market farm woes" (9 October 1984, 14). In the United States, "Amid bumper crops, farmers fight to hang on," the *U.S. News & World Report* reported in 1982, pointing out that "rural incomes are plummeting as fast as record harvests are pouring in; yet, while most farmers are hurting, few of them are ready to give up" (1 November, 72).

Explaining why farmers are in such straits when their harvests are bounteous is beyond the scope of this book (and, I confess, the scope of my understanding). But explanations as to why crops are called "bumper" when there is more of a harvest than usual is quite at home here.

First of all, *bumper* has nothing to do with bumping, or colliding. For that we have a car bumper or fender. With respect to grain, *bumper* has retained its original ties with agriculture, although indirectly, for a bumper was originally a full glass of ale, as noted in this excerpt from a seventeenth century ballad:

> For the Liquor of life we do dearly adore,
> When the bottles are empty we'll thunder for more,
> For to make our hearts chearful we'll merrily sing
> With a rousing full Bumper to Caesar, our King.

By the eighteenth century, the English, who had invented the word, forgot why their ancestors had referred to a full glass as a bumper. One of the common explanations of the day was that the word was derived from a Catholic custom in which people toasted the Pope with a drink dedicated to "au bon Pere," French for "to the good father." While this was widely believed to be the origin of the word, it was not, since the Pope was not called "bon Pere" but rather "saint Pere," the "holy Father."

The answer lies not in the sacred, but in the very profane subject of war. During the Middle Ages, a large cannon was called a *bombard,* from the Latin *bombardus,* "a great gun." To some imaginative word-coiner, there was a certain similarity between the destruction spilling out from the mouth of the cannon and that from the rim of a large glass of ale. Large bottles for ale were also called bombards for the same reason (*see* Bumboat).

In Shakespeare's time, *bumbard* was already slang for drunkard, as reflected in the *Tempest* (2.2.21): "Yond' same black cloud, yond' huge one, looks like a foul bumbard that would shed his liquor." Since the letter *b* and *p* were (and still are) readily interchanged, bumbard some time later was transformed into *bumpard* and from that into *bumper*. So when the farmer talks of a bumper crop, he means that he has more than enough to fill his silo, an allusion to a word that centuries ago also meant full, then, however, with respect to a glass of ale.

Bumper can also refer to any situation where there is more of something than usual. The Toronto *Globe and Mail* (28 February 1983, 7), for instance, referred to a "bumper of Tory myths," while on the other side of the North American continent the *Los Angeles Times* (16 April 1984, 1.1) carried the headline: "Bumper crop of bankruptcies: 100,000 face foreclosures as deepening credit crisis dramatically changes rural life style." Back on the East Coast, the *Christian Science Monitor* was noting that "In London, [1983 was] a bumper year for tourists—and swindlers."

Butler

The *butler* is a valet, a personal servant, a "gentleman's gentleman." He is often a respected and highly regarded employee working for a very wealthy employer. A butler's appearance is very important. Generally he wears formal evening clothes while on duty. Until the last century he would try to appear slightly less formally dressed than his employer. Around the turn of the present century, however, those who could afford butlers started to dress less formally, while their butlers retained their more formal appearance. Once you could tell who was butler and who was "gentleman" by picking out the better dressed of the two. Now the opposite is true.

Books and movies abound with famous butlers. Hudson was the stern Scottish butler in the popular TV series of the 1970s and '80s, "Upstairs, Downstairs." Jeeves, created by P. G. Wodehouse, is another famous manservant. Wodehouse introduced the character in his book *Jeeves Takes Charge* and, true to butler's origins as a servant in charge of the wine cellar (which we'll see in a moment),

Jeeves is hired because of his cure for hangover. Jeeves assesses Bertie Wooster's condition and instantly knows what to do. Going to the kitchen, he returns shortly with a glass:

> "If you would drink this, sir," he said, with a kind bedside manner rather like a royal doctor shooting the bracer into the sick prince. "It is a little preparation of my own invention. It is the Worcester sauce that gives it its color. The raw egg makes it nutritious. The red pepper gives it its bite. Gentlemen have told me they have found it extremely invigorating after a late evening."
>
> I would have clutched at anything that looked like a lifeline that morning. I swallowed the stuff. For a moment I felt as if somebody had touched off a bomb inside the old bean and was strolling down my throat with a light torch, then everything seemed suddenly to get all right. The sun shone in through the window; birds twittered in the tree-tops; and, generally speaking, hope dawned once more . . . .

And Jeeves had a job.

The erstwhile "bottler"-turned-manservant has also been the devious murderer in many mystery stories, and "the butler did it" was once a cliché among mystery fans. Butlers have also been the sidekicks to detectives like Lord Peter Wimsey, Dorothy Sayers' famous English sleuth. Sayers, incidentally, owed her surname to the assayers of old whose job it was to taste their lord's wine to determine if it were poisoned.

Suave and sophisticated through the modern butler may be, his predecessors were often menial employees in large homes owned by nobility. The word itself and the surname *Butler* are derived from the part of the household where this servant generally worked, the *buttery*. This was not a storage area for butter, akin to the larder where lard was stored, or the pantry where bread (Latin *panis*) was kept; rather, the buttery was originally the place where the *butts*—or bottled wine—were stored: "Bid my subsizer carry my hackney to the buttery, and give him his bever; it is a civil and sober beast, and will drink moderately (Beaumont and Fletcher, *The Elder Brother,* 1637, 710).

Later the buttery was also used to designate the room where other provisions for a large household were kept. A less exalted servant, but one who also worked in or was in charge of the buttery, was the *despencer,* the person who kept the buttery well stocked with wine and other provisions. Descendants of these servants are the *Spences* and the *Spencers.*

Since he was in charge of the bottles, the butler was first known as the *bottler,* a word that comes from French *bouteille,* "bottle." His official position was *bouteillier,* "the servant in charge of the bottles." The fact that French was the language spoken by the educated in England until the fourteenth century, whereas the lower classes spoke English, accounts for the French origin of so many English occupational surnames such as Butler. Nor is this French emphasis surprising, since the people who conquered England spoke French and naturally retained their native language after they settled in England.

It was the butler's duty to look after the wine cellar (buttery) where the bottles were kept. In some cases, he was also in charge of importing wine so that the household would always have its supply.

The butler's job and the tendency of some in this position to sometimes sample what they served comes through in this amusing poem by the sixteenth century writer, John Heywood:

> The butler and the beer horse both be like one:
> They draw beer both; that is truth to bide one.
> Both draw beer, indeed, but yet they differ, Joan;
> The butler draweth and drinketh beer, the horse drinketh none.

In some households, however, the butler's job, though still associated with wine, was not menial at all in the sense of low status. He was, rather, the servant who personally attended the nobleman or king during his dinner, at which times he poured his master's wine.

According to Reaney and Wilson's *Dictionary of British Surnames* (1977), the first recorded use of Butler as a surname is that of Hugo Buteiller—Hugo the Butler—mentioned in 1055. Although butlers haven't exactly gone the way of the slide rule, relatively few are still employed in that capacity. Nevertheless, you can get some idea of just how many butlers were once in England by looking at the *London Telephone Directory* and tallying the various surnames. Among the hundreds of surnames denoting occupations, Butler is sixteenth, and nine columns are required to list the 977 citations appearing in the 1984 edition.

While butlering has almost disappeared in England except in the wealthiest of households, butlers are still in demand, especially in the United States where some earn as much as $30,000 in addition to free room and board. The modern-day training ground for these household servants is the School of Butlers in London, which charges £2,000 ($2,800 at the present exchange) for a two-month course. In 1985, history was made when the first woman butler took her place among the distinguished graduating class. (*See also* Assay *and* Brewster.)

Cakes and ale

Before *beer and skittles* was the popular British expression for revelry, Britons cherished their *cakes and ale*. This is possibly the best-known expression in Shakespeare's *Twelfth Night* (2.3.124), where abstemious Malvolio is berated by the fun-loving sot Sir Toby Belch: "Dost thou think, because thou art virtuous, there shall be no more cakes and ale?" Several centuries later in 1930, Somerset Maugham used the expression as the title of a book in which he lampooned the English author Thomas Hardy.

Canteen

A canteen is either a cloth-covered flask used by campers or soldiers for carrying water or other liquids, or it is a place on a military post where soldiers can relax and refresh themselves or buy extra provisions. Both connotations derive from the Italian *cantina,* a "wine cellar." *Cantina* passed into Spanish without change, and when Americans moved into the Southwest, they simply adopted this term, corrupted to *canteen,* for a saloon.

The current association of canteen with drinking obviously stems from its Italian origin, and men who drank from the same canteen felt a special bond of friendship for one another:

> There are bonds of all sorts in this world of ours,
> Letters of friendship and ties of flowers,
> But there's never a bond, old friend, like this,
> We have drunk from the same canteen.
>
> (C. G. Halpine, *The Canteen*)

Cellar, cellarer, cellarette

When I was a boy I explored every nook and cranny of my home—except for the *cellar.* I would hide from my parents in the attic, in the closets, under the bed . . . but never in the cellar.

For me the cellar contained unknown terrors. It was dark and damp, and monsters lurked in the shadows, waiting to pounce on me and take me to wherever it is that monsters take children foolish enough to enter their dens.

Kids growing up in suburbia no longer know what a cellar is. The room below the kitchen is now the "rec" room, and it is usually brimming with toys, bikes, a ping pong table, and just plain junk.

The cellar of bygone years was also a storeroom, a cool part of the house below ground level. Before the icebox and the refrigerator, this was where food was kept to delay spoilage.

Cellar comes from Latin *cella,* meaning "a set of cells." In some cellars, these cells were wine bottles or barrels of wine, and the storage area itself was called a wine cellar. By extension (actually metonomy), wine was sometimes synonymous with cellar, as in the expression, "his cellar is renown," or with a case containing wine or liquor bottles. That indefatigable diarist, Samuel Pepys, noted in his entry for 1 April 1668 that the wife of a friend gave Pepys "a cellar of waters of her own distilling." In Italy a wine cellar was called a *cantina* which gave rise to canteen.

Americans may not be the world's biggest wine drinkers, but they probably have more wine cellars than any other nation. Or at least they seem obsessed about owning a wine cellar, if the amount of space devoted to the subject by American magazines is a fair criterion.

Fortune magazine (June 1967, 122) maintained with no hesitation that "good living begins in the wine cellar." An article in *San Francisco* magazine (September 1984, 40) advised readers about "starting your own wine cellar for under $500." Ah, inflation: Eleven years earlier *House and Garden* told readers how to start "a good wine cellar for less than $100," and four years before that the same magazine advised them "how to plan a $50 wine cellar." In a "yuppier" economic environment, *Signature Magazine* (August 1986) described the perfect wine cellar as one storing 267 bottles of premium varietals selling for between $7 and $15 each!

A few years earlier, *Working Woman* (December 1983, 129) gave advice on "setting up a wine cellar." If your home does not allow for an underground cellar, *Popular Science* (September 1983, 64) had advice on "two kitchen dividers that bring the wine cellar upstairs." If a kitchen divider is not to your liking, *Library Journal* (September 1978, 10) offered "happiness [by] turning the nursery into a wine cellar . . . when the offspring have sprung."

After setting it up, above ground or below, *House Beautiful* (February 1979, 114) told you "how to stock a wine cellar," and if you couldn't wait for your wine to age, *Vogue* had all you needed to know about "a cellar you can drink from now." Cost conscious? *Sunset* (October 1978, 146) described what to do for an "energy-efficient wine cellar."

Centuries ago, if an estate or a monastery had a wine cellar, it also had a special servant to look after it. This servant was someone known either as a *cellarer* or *butler*. The butler eventually became an upstairs servant, while the cellarer remained downstairs. It was his job to inspect all the casks of wine in the cellar, including funnels and spigots. If the wine had become discolored, he added coloring; if weakened, he added spices. He also made special spice-wines as requested by the master. In more modest settings, the owner was his own cellarer and took a certain pride in stocking vintage wines: "I shall remember . . . whenever I have the pleasure of entertaining you, that I am the cellarer of that wine," says one of the characters in George Meredith's novel, *The Egoist* (ch. 20). When importing and selling wine became a middle-class business, a wine merchant was also known as a cellarer.

Today the cellarer is known as a *sommelier* in posh hotels and better restaurants, but Ray Wellington, sommelier at Windows on the World in New York City, says he prefers the term *cellar master* (*New York Times,* 28 March 1984, C.1). As in the past, the sommelier or cellar master is responsible for keeping the establishment's wine cellar full and properly stocked with vintage and house wines; in addition, he is the resident expert on which wine to serve with what. For some patrons he may also decant the wine, a gesture that does not come cheap, however, tips ranging from $10 to $15 for this service alone during a dinner.

On a wine-making estate, the cellar master's job is to clarify the wine before it is filtered. The trademark or symbol of the cellar master, whether he works upstairs or down, is a little cup called a *tastevin,* which is worn around the neck. For the restaurant cellar master, this is purely a ceremonial trinket. The downstairs cellar master, on the other hand, actually uses it to give prospective wine brokers a taste of the estate's wares.

During the eighteenth century, a movable wine cellar, called a cellarette, was a fashionable piece of furniture in well-to-do homes. It was usually made of mahogany and was lined inside with metal. The interior was divided into cells for wine bottles, and the base was sometimes fitted with a board that slid out so it could be used as table for pouring the wine. Cellarettes were also known as *garde-vines,* a Scottish and then Americanized version of the French *garde de vin,* "keeper of the wine." *(See also* Butler *and* Canteen.*)*

"Good night, Mrs. Calabash, wherever you are."

With those parting words, the great "Schnozzola," Jimmy Durante, waved good-bye to his audience and walked out of the spotlight into the darkness of the stage. Durante never revealed who Mrs. Calabash was or why he singled her out from all his legions of admirers. Every time there was a new woman in his life, the gossip columnists wondered if at long last they had solved the mystery. But no one ever did. They couldn't have. She did not exist except in Durante's playful imagination.

The "Schnozzola" started his career before the turn of the century in Tony's Saloon on Coney Island and spent many years playing in saloons even after stardom. The *Mrs. Calabash* of Durante's formative years was a long-necked, oval-shaped whiskey bottle with the collar at its base. These bottles were commonplace in the United States after 1850 and were often kept as decorations in American homes because picturesque historical symbols, emblems, portraits of national heroes and other figures were imprinted on them. Homes that could not afford paintings had calabash bottles for art.

One of the most popular calabash engravings was of Jenny Lind, the "Swedish nightingale." Jenny Lind was a world famous soprano of the mid-1800s who sang in every major opera house in Europe. She was brought to America in 1850 by another famous showman, P. T. Barnum, who took her on a cross-country concert tour. Americans were enchanted by her voice. Poems were written in her honor, and newspapers reported her every appearance. So well known did she become that calabash makers etched her face on their bottles along with portraits of national heroes and presidents.

Was Mrs. Calabash merely a liquor bottle? Or could she have been the famous Jenny Lind whose face and features Durante stared at in saloons night after night during the early years of his career? Only Jimmy Durante knew.

Carouse

A *carousal* is a noisy party. It is not to be confused with its lookalike, carousel. The latter is a merry-go-round, and the word derives from the Italian *carosello,* "a tournament."

A *carouse* was originally a large drink or a round of drinks, and a *carousal* was a boisterous celebration due to all the drinking or carousing being done.

Two possible derivations have been suggested for *carouse.* The first is that it comes from the German *gar,* "completely," and *aus,* "out." *Garaustrinken* in German means to "drink it all," to "drain the glass"; thus *gar aus* was the German equivalent of our "bottoms up." From German the expression passed into French as *carrousse* and from there into English as *carouse.* The *Oxford English Dictionary* dates the word's earliest appearance in the language in the late 1500s. A second derivation traces its origins to Danish *rouse,* a large glass in which toasts were made. Based on this source, *carouse* originally meant to refill a *rouse.*

A cask savors of its first fill.

The wine *cask* figures in many proverbs. One of the oldest was first coined or reported by the Roman poet Horace: "A cask will long retain the odor with which it was first imbued" (*Epistles* 1.2.69). Variations on the theme are found in the biblical, "Train up a child in the way he should go, and when he is old he will not depart from it"

(Proverbs 22:6); Alexander Pope's "as the twig is bent, the tree is inclined"; and William Wordsworth's "The child is father to the man."

"You can take the boy out of the country, but you can't take the country out of the boy" is the Americanized version. It means that our early environment—the home we are raised in, the friends we associate with, the values of the community we live in—all determine how we will think and behave later in life.

Orthodox Freudian psychology lives by these proverbs. The child is cask; his experiences, wine. What the proverbs and the Freudians fail to consider is that not only does wine not affect each cask in the same way, but the cask itself affects the wine.

Take bourbon whiskey for example.

This native American whiskey was invented by a Kentucky preacher, the Reverend Elija Craig. It was not a deliberate invention in the "99 percent perspiration, 1 percent inspiration" Edison tradition, but an accidental one. In 1789, Craig was heating staves of white oak to age them for some barrels. Called away by some emergency, he left the staves in the fire too long and they charred. Not one to throw anything away, he scraped the blackened surfaces and fashioned them into barrels anyway. Then he poured his whiskey into the barrels. Later when he sampled it, his whiskey tasted mellower and less harsh than any whiskey he had previously produced. From then on Reverend Craig charred his staves on purpose.

Bourbon can be made from corn or rye or any other grain, but for bourbon to be bourbon it must have been stored in charred oak barrels for at least two years.

If aging in a charred oak barrel improves the flavor of whiskey, what would happen if whiskey were to spend part of the aging process in other kinds of wood? This is what George Dickel wondered soon after settling in the Cumberland hills of southern Tennessee in 1870. Dickel had learned distilling in his native Germany and had settled in that part of Tennessee because of the water, which was naturally filtered through limestone. Soon after setting up his distillery he began experimenting with the effects of different woods on whiskey and finally devised his own special technique. First he fermented mash in tanks made of cypress wood. Next he transferred the fermented whiskey into mellowing tanks made of yellow poplar containing charcoal made from sugar maple. The third stage involved aging the whiskey in charred white-oak barrels.

So while it's true that "a cask savors of its first fill," it is also true that the cask itself affects what is put into it.

Cocksure

Cocksure means overly confident, self-assured. For a word with such a meaning you would expect a flawless pedigree. Quite the opposite is true, however. No one knows for sure where the word came from; as a result, there are plenty of theories.

One theory relates it to the strutting rooster, the cock of the chicken farm. A second contends it comes from the cock on a firelock. The venerable *Oxford English Dictionary* sees a connection to alcohol and suggests that it refers "to the security, or certainty of the action of a cock or tap in preventing the escape of liquor." The OED also points to "lecherous" as another meaning of the word. Alfred Holt in *Phrase and Word Origins* calls this connotation obsolete. He could not help adding, however: "In a way, that's unfortunate, as we could have explained that one."

Cocktail, cocktail belt, cocktail hour

A cocktail is any mixed drink made with one or more alcoholic beverages such as whiskey, rum, gin, brandy, vodka, wine, beer, and so forth, and juices, flavorings, other beverages, or water. It is typically served in a glass over shaved ice.

From its specific and mundane meaning, *cocktail* has now become a generic term for any mixture of chemicals. Referring to a new cancer treatment in which patients receive several drugs simultaneously, the *New Scientist* on 31 January 1985 reported that initial trials with such "cocktails" of the most potent anti-cancer drugs [had] little effect on inhibiting the growth and spread of melanotic tumour cells" (p. 19). Less sublime is the favorite concoction of terrorists around the world—the "Molotov cocktail." This is an incendiary device which is hurled at a target from a short distance. It gets its explosive power from gasoline and a burning wick.

According to C. K. Ogden *(The System of Basic English,* 134), *cocktail* is among the fifty best-known words in the English language. Three others on the list are *alcohol, bar* and *beer!* The history of a word of such international stature deserves to be heralded. Unfortunately, there is more speculation than certainty behind this most popular of the world's potations.

The cocktail is generally conceded to be an American invention. Washington Irving wrote that Maryland was the home of the cocktail as well as several other alcoholic drinks: "[The citizens of Maryland] lay claim to be the first inventor of these recondite beverages, cock-tail, stone-fence, and sherry-cobbler" *(History of New York,* 1809). Three years earlier on 13 May 1806, a Hudson, New York, newspaper, *The Balance* reported that the "cock tail is a stimulating liquor, composed of spirits of any kind, sugar, water, and bitters—it is vulgarly called bittered sling, and is supposed to be an excellent electioneering potion" (p. 146).

Whatever the origin of the word, there are now literally thousands of formulas that go by the name cocktail. H. L. Mencken said that he once employed a mathematician to figure out how many variations of this *materia bibulica* were possible; 17,864,392,788 was the figure arrived at. "We tried 273 at random," he says, "and found them all good, though some, of course, were better than others" *(The American Language,* Supplement 1, 1945, 260).

Although the *cocktail bar* or *cocktail lounge* were familiar sights to Mencken, he does not seem to have been aware of an American institution that emerged during the 1920s and is still popular today—the *cocktail hour*. In clock time this usually involves the hours between 6:00 and 8:00 P.M. During Prohibition, parties of men and women (known as the "smart set") would gather outside a popular speakeasy, whisper a secret password ("Al Capone sent me," for example) and rush in to drink prodigiously before going out for dinner. After Prohibition, the party atmosphere changed, but the custom of having a cocktail before dinner was firmly established. When "suburbanization" erupted across America in the 1950s, the cocktail hour became a fixture of the *cocktail belt,* a name given to those new developments populated mostly by upwardly mobile, cocktail-drinking executives and their families.

In the American fashion, the cocktail has spawned its own special cult and culture. A cocktail is served at a cocktail lounge in a cocktail glass from a cocktail tray by a cocktail waitress to someone sitting at a cocktail table. While sipping the cocktail, the customer may or may not be aware of the cocktail pianist playing background music on his cocktail piano or the sound of another drink being prepared at the bar in a cocktail shaker. If he has been invited to someone's home and arrives about 7:00 P.M. during the middle of the cocktail hour, he may find himself at a cocktail party surrounded by women in cocktail dresses or cocktail gowns. Before sipping his cocktail, he may remove the small cocktail onion from the cocktail stick garnishing his drink, drain his glass, and go to the table to satisfy his hunger with a few cocktail sausages. And if he cocktails too much and gets cocktailed, he may regret his cocktailing the following day.

Codswallop

This is another word for nonsense, ridiculous, farfetched, baloney, and the like. It is thought to be an eponymous word, the first syllable allegedly named for an American inventor, Hiram Codd, who in 1875 patented a bottle to keep the fizz in mineral water. (Its secret was a marble-like stopper.) The second part, *wallop,* was a slang term for beer, something no one would ever want to put into Codd's bottle. *Codswallop* then was someting utterly silly. These are its origins according to Brewer's *Dictionary of Phrase and Fable;* Boycott's *Batty, Bloomers and Boycott; Reader's Digest's Strange Stories, Amazing Fact.* But they're all mistaken.

Codswallop is not listed in Farmer and Henley's encyclopedic *Slang and Its Analogues,* or in Webster's *Dictionary of American Slang.* It is also not in Eric Partridge's 1970 slang dictionary, but it does appear in the 1984 revision of Partridge's dictionary by Paul Beale, who says that it was in general use around 1930 in phrases like "a load of cod's wallop."

Since *codswallop* is not listed in American dictionaries but is sometimes encountered in English dictionaries, the eponymous explanation is probably mistaken. More probably, *codswallop,* like its cousin *balderdash,* is a product of England, not America. Although the *Oxford English Dictionary* did not originally list *codswallop,* it was included in its Supplement. Four references are given, the earliest being 1963. With English origin the *cod* in *codswallop*—as encountered in English slang—refers to testicles. This suggests that codswallop had nothing at all to do with Hiram Codd or with beer. It is merely an emphatic "Balls!" With such earthy words as "balls" or "bullshit" available, it's no wonder that we rarely hear or read *codswallop* anywhere. But if *bullshit* offends you and you're tired of *baloney, fiddlesticks* or *balderdash,* try it. At worst you'll only get a puzzled look and a "Huh?" You certainly won't get a bottle of beer.

Crappy

If you've ever answered "crappy" to a question about how you're feeling, you've probably described an unpleasant woozy, nauseous, unsettling sensation that has less to do with your bowel than with your head. The *crappy* feeling comes from *crapulous* or *crapulence,* old words for "hangover," dating back to the sixteenth century. Related to these is *crapper,* "a half glassful of whiskey." Each of these is derived from Latin *crapula,* which in turn comes from Greek *kraipale,* "drunken sickness."

On the other hand, if someone asked you what you thought of a play you had just seen or the date you just had and you answered "crappy," meaning inferior, less than acceptable, unpalatable, or substandard in any way, then excrement was the sense intended. This crappy comes from *crap,* "to defecate," and is eponymously derived from Thomas Crapper, the inventor of the flush toilet, first called "Crapper's Valveless Water Waste Preventor. Expressions like *load of crap* and *full of crap* are cognates. Not so, *crap out,* meaning "to lose," especially to lose money in a *crap game.* The latter comes from another eponymous source, John Crapaud, nickname of a French gambler, Bernard Marigny, who in the early 1800s showed New Orleans a new way to play with dice.

Credenza, cupboard

A *credenza* is a small table on which food or drinks are placed. It comes from German *credenzen,* "to pour out," which in turn is derived from Latin *credentia,* "trust or belief." Other related words are *credibility* and *credentials.* The *credence-table* got its name from the practice of placing food or drink on a special table so that it could be tasted by a servant known as an assayer to determine that it did not contain poison before serving it to the lord of a manor. The testing itself was called *credence.*

The Roman Catholic and Anglican churches have for their liturgies a counterpart to the profane credence-table, not to protect anyone from being poisoned, but to offer credence—belief or faith in the symbolism of the communion. The credence-table is usually located to the right of the altar. On it are placed the bread and wine, cruets, washing basin, and napkin used in the ablutions.

A more commonplace piece of furniture which also has its origins in the poisoning plots of by-gone centuries is the *cupboard.* When poisoning ceased to be a popular means of doing away with one's family, the credence-table became a cupboard, a piece of furniture on which gold and silver cups and plates were displayed. In homes of more modest means, this cupboard became a cabinet with shelves, called a *short-cupboard.* In such a piece of furniture a family's prized earthenware cups and plates were exhibited. In still more modest homes, the cupboard became a place for keeping the everyday cups and saucers, glasses and plates, or it was a special area reserved for alcoholic beverages. *(See also* Assay.*)*

Cute

Babies, puppies, kittens—almost any of God's creatures will invariably be called "cute" at some time or another during their infancies. Some are "cute as a bug's ear" or "cute as a button." I've never seen a nice looking ear on a bug or on any living thing for that matter. Ears aren't cute, they're just there. As for buttons—what's so cute about a button? A button is plain or ornate. Not cute. Teenage girls used to call good-looking boys cute. Now they call them "hunks." Girls were once called cuties or cutie pies.

Some etymologists look to *acute* for the origin of the word and contend that it means "sharp" or "clever." But in each of the above uses the word means winsome, nice looking, attractive, sweet. How can anyone think a baby or a puppy clever?

No. *Cute* means pleasing, and that's where its beginnings lie. It is not from *acute* but directly from Middle English *cute,* which itself came from Middle French *cuit* via Latin *coquere* "to boil wine." During Greek and Roman times, as well as the Middle Ages, grape juice was boiled to evaporate some of the water; it was then sweetened to mask the acid taste. This boiling and sweetening was collectively called "making the wine cute." By extension, anything sweetened was cute.

Dead marine

A *dead marine* is an empty bottle of some alcoholic beverage. The expression goes back at least to 1785 where it appeared in Francis Grose's *Dictionary of the Vulgar Tongue*.

According to British lore, William IV, Lord High Admiral of the British Navy, is said to have pointed to some empty bottles and ordered a waiter, "Take away those marines!"

An elderly officer of the Marines at the same dinner took offense at the remark. "Sir, you have slurred a branch of Her Majesty's service to which I proudly belong by associating empty bottles with marines."

The Admiral, who was generally very tactful, realizing he had angered the marine officer, extricated himself from what was becoming an embarrassing situation by explaining, "I call them marines, sir, because they are good fellows who have done their duty and are now ready to do it again!"

Despite the Admiral's nimble thinking, the expression stuck, possibly because there was widespread unfavorable opinion of marines in the sixteenth century when the Marines were a feeble branch of the services compared to Britain's Navy with its able-bodied seamen.

Debauch, debauchery, debaucher, debauchee

During the Middle Ages men needed a skill if they were to earn a living. Many years of apprenticeship had to be served before one could qualify as a recognized craftsman.

After serving his apprenticeship a craftsman would open a small shop called a *bauche* in French. If business prospered he might take on helpers.

Not everyone either could or wished to work all the time, however, and assistants often looked for opportunities to get together for a good time. Not wanting to carouse alone they tried to persuade their friends to join them. Those who were persuaded were said to have been "debauché" (from French *de* "from" and *bauche* "shop." Literally they were "lured away from the shop."

Debauché was Anglicized to *debauched* when it entered English in the late 1500s and kept its meaning of enticement away from something or someone, like a soldier from his post or a wife from her husband. In his diary entry for 3 July 1667, Samuel Pepys mentions two young men who were debauched into stealing their fathers' clothes. But the most common sense of the word usually involves physical depravity such as excessive drinking or sexual seduction:

> The Delights of the Bottle, and charms of good Wine
> To the power and pleasures of Love must resign;
> Though the nights in the joys of good drinking be past
> The debauches but till the morning will last;
> But Love's great debauch is more lasting and strong
> For that often lasts a man all his life long.

"The Delights of the Bottle," *Roxburghe Ballads* (vol. 4, 2.45)

Dionysian. *See* Bacchic

Dithyrambic. *See* Bacchic

Delirium tremens

One of the most unpleasant and dangerous aspects of withdrawal from alcohol is a condition known as *delirium tremens*—the D.T.s. In this state it is not unusual to hallucinate so badly that insects or animals seem to be crawling up and down one's body or under one's skin.

The word *delirium* refers to a wandering of the mind. But originally it had a more mundane meaning, based on its Latin roots, *de* "from" and *lira* "furrow." Combined, these two words gave the Romans *delirare,* "to depart from a furrow." Our word *delirium* also refers to a departure, not from plowing or other work but from the "furrow" of the mind. *Tremens* comes from Latin *tremere,* "to tremble," in the sense of "be afraid of."

Delirium tremens was coined in 1813 by Thomas S. Sutton, an English physician who used it in the title of a book, *Tracts on Delirium Tremens.* Before and since, there have been many other less academic ways of referring to this condition, among which are:

barrel fever	rams
bats	rats
black dog	rum fit
blue devils	screaming Abdams
blue horrors	screaming meanies
bottle ache	seeing pink elephants
gallon distemper	seeing snakes
heeby jeebies	shakes
horrors	shim-shams
jerks	snake in the boots
jim-jams	uglies
jimmies	whammy
jumps	whoops and jingles
ork-orks	zings

Distill

Distill comes from Latin *stilla,* "drip or drop," and the prefix *de,* "from." Literally it means to trickle down in drops. The Latin verb *distilare,* "to form from drops," passed almost unchanged into English as *distill* and *distillation.* Distillation is a process in which a fluid is first vaporized by heat, condensed into drops by cooling, and then collected by a container.

Our word *distillery* is first encountered in Chaucer's writings dating to the late fourteenth century, but the distillation process was well known centuries before among the ancient Egyptians.

The Egyptians had a crude but effective method of separating fluids by distillation using a "box still." This was simply an airtight box containing a bowl with some liquid. A glass-like cover was slanted across the box. When the box was placed in the hot sun, the liquid would vaporize, come in contact with the slanted lid, and form drops which ran down the side into a trough. It took Europe a thousand years to rediscover the process.

Just as distillation of alcohol is strictly under government control today, in Egyptian times only priests and the nobility were licensed to operate a still. This meant that distillation remained a secret in Egyptian society, and later it continued to be a secret among the Arabs who refined the process and developed the alembic—a container with a round head and spout called a beak. Instead of vaporized drops collecting on a flat plate, the alembic kept the vapor from escaping and channeled it into the beak. The beak led into a condensing coil at the end of which the drops were collected. In the fourteenth century the alchemist-physician Arnold of Villanova mastered the process and taught it to Europeans. And the secret was no more. *(See also* Alcohol.*)*

Dregs of society

"We're getting rid of the dregs left over from Christmas," said a store manager in an interview with a reporter from *U.S. News & World Report* (28 January 1985, 63). In a time of management-labor unrest, one might suppose that these "dregs" were employees who the store manager felt had not done their best to boost holiday sales. But no, the shop's dregs were the large inventory of unsold goods. To get rid of these dregs, which weeks before he had heralded as valuable amenities, if not necessities, the store manager was offering them at large discounts.

Originally *dregs* referred to the sediment that forms at the bottom of a wine cask after it has been standing for some time. This sediment is also called *lees*. From this specific meaning of refuse or worthless residue, dregs took on metaphorical garb and as early as 1546 was applied to vile and despicable people. Nowadays these bottom-of-the-barrel types are often called "dregs of society," to be deliberately discarded like refuse or waste matter.

The dregs of society are never singular. No one ever describes another person, no matter how loathesome, as a "dreg of society" (although in *Troilus and Creseida* [3.2.65] Shakespeare calls one of his characters a dreg). You can be called *dreggish* or *dreggy,* but not *a* dreg. Refuse always comes in clumps.

Drunk

"In American slang," writes Gary Jennings in *World of Words,* "the three topics which have engendered the greatest number of expressions, whether admiring or disparaging, are drinking, love and money—in that order" (p. 93). The *Dictionary of American Slang* makes the same point: "The concept having the most slang synonyms is drunk." The compilers list 353 terms for drunk, commenting that "this vast number of drunk words does not necessarily mean that Americans are obsessed with drinking, though we seem obsessed with talking about it" (p. 652).

The earliest list of words for drunk was compiled and published by Benjamin Franklin in the *Pennsylvania Gazette* on 6 January 1737. The following April it was reprinted in the *South Carolina Gazette.* The list contained 228 words or phrases, covered one and a half pages of both newspapers, and bore the heading: "The Drinkers Dictionary." It began with an aphorism Franklin had previously written in his *Poor Richard's Almanac:* "Nothing more like a Fool than a drunken Man," and concluded with a brief statement about his sources for compiling the list, including his feelings about drunkenness:

> The Phrases in this Dictionary are not (like most of our Terms of Art) borrow'd from Foreign Languages, neither are they collected from the writings of the Learned in our own, but gather'd wholly from the modern Tavern-Conversation of Tipplers. I do not doubt but that there are many more in use; and I was even tempted to add a new one myself under the Letter B, to wit, Brutify'd: But upon Consideration, I fear'd being guilty of Injustice to the Brute Creation, if I represented Drunkenness as a beastly Vice, since, 'tis well-known, that the Brutes are in general a very sober sort of People.

In the December 1770 issue of *Gentleman's Magazine* an anonymous writer in England compiled his own list of 78 words and phrases for drunk (some of them identical to Franklin's) and speculated why people got drunk and why so many euphemisms, circumlocutions and synonyms existed for the condition:

> If in the general estimation the substitution of frenzy for reason is desirable, it follows, that in the general estimation it is advantageous to exchange what is, for what is not. This, however, like most other gratifications, has been stigmatized as immoral, and indeed with much better reason than many, for upon the whole, it certainly lessens the good of life, however small, and encreases the evil, however great. We have therefore contrived a great variety of names and phrases, most of them whimsical and ludicrous, to veil the turpitude of what is pleasing in itself, and generally connected with reciprocations, if not of friendship, yet of the lesser duties and endearments of society.

Another list of 105 words and phrases was compiled in 1927 by Edmund Wilson as a "lexicon of Prohibition." Four years later an article entitled "Volstead English" appeared in *American Speech,* listing 108 words the author claimed had been spawned by Prohibition. Eight of them, however, had appeared in the *Pennsylvania Gazette* or *Gentleman's Magazine* nearly 200 years earlier.

When *The American Thesaurus of Slang* appeared in 1953, it listed almost 900 words for drunk. In 1981, Richard Spears, a professor of linguistics at Northwestern University, in *Slang and Euphemism,* compiled 908. "Certainly no human being has a vocabulary including all of them," says Spears. By far the longest list to date is Paul Dickson's 2,231 synonyms covering 45 pages of his book *Words.* (See Appendix for my own list.)

Why then are there so many words for drunk?

The unknown author in *Gentleman's Magazine* contended that our drunk vocabulary is nothing less than a mirror of our shame and immorality. We do not want to admit, and thus we "veil our turpitude," he concluded. In *I Hear America Talking* Stuart Flexner argues that people get drunk for many different reasons and being drunk affects people in a variety of ways. Our vast lexicon of drunk slang merely reflects these many feelings and reactions, says Flexner.

But the same could be said for pain. People feel pain for different reasons. It can be caused by a boat, car, train, or plane accident. When you were a child you probably fell down the stairs, scraped your elbow or your knee or your face. You were probably spanked or sent to your room. You have probably been teased, been in a fight, fallen from a tree. All caused pain. Why then is there not as richly endowed a vocabulary for pain, if pain, like drunk, is mainly a reflection of feelings and reactions?

I don't know.

Dr. Harry Gene Levine of the Department of Sociology at the City University of New York is another who has wondered, and he too does not know. "Obviously," writes Levine, "Americans, like many other peoples of the world, have taken being drunk very seriously. Alcohol researchers, however, have not—they have never seriously examined normal, ordinary, nonpathological drunkenness; the drunkenness of parties and celebrations, of beginnings and endings, and of mourning. The various words for drunk are data on the meaning of drunkenness in American culture, and the interpretations of items appear to be wide open" *(Journal of Studies on Alcohol,* vol. 42, 1038).

There you are, all you aspiring Ph.D.s in sociology or psychology or alcohology. Here's a topic where you'll find no competition.

You can start with the *Oxford English Dictionary* which traces *drunk* back to 800 when it appeared as *drync,* the *u* in early Middle English being equivalent to Old English *y.* Later variants include *druuncen* (950), *druncena* (1050), *drunke* (1340), and *dronke* (1450). By the late sixteenth century *drunk* had taken its present form.

Another possibility for our aspiring candidate would be to gather and research the various similes involving drunk. What follows is a partial list, with dates of first appearance and some commentary that could no doubt be expanded:

drunk as an ape: early fourteenth century. One of the earliest recorded "drunk as. . . ." Found in Chaucer's "The Manciple's Tale," 1:44: "Ther to me thynketh ye ben wel yshape. I trowe that ye dronken han wyn ape." Another early "Drunk as. . ." is also Chaucer's: "drunk as a maus." (See below.)

drunk as Bacchus: the god of wine

drunk as a badger

drunk as the Baltic: nineteenth century

drunk as a bastard

drunk as a bat

drunk as a beast: nineteenth century

drunk as a beggar: seventeenth century

drunk as a besom

drunk as a billy goat

drunk as a boiled owl

drunk as a brewer's fart

drunk as a broom

drunk as Chloe: nineteenth century. Apparently a real person, Chloe, the wife of a cobbler in England, was known for her drinking habits. Nevertheless, the poet Prior was enamored of her.

drunk as a cook
drunk as a coon
drunk as a coot
drunk as a cunt

drunk as David's Sow: seventeenth century. Allegedly from an incident in the life of David Lloyd, an alehouse keeper in Hereford. Lloyd had a sow with six legs which he used as an attraction for his alehouse. Unfortunately, he also had a wife who liked her ale "for which he used sometimes to give her correction." One day Lloyd's wife drank too much (but not so much that she was oblivious of the consequences), and she decided to hide while sleeping it off. The safest place to do so, she decided, was in the pig's pen, and she chased the sow out and lay down in its place.

In the meantime, a group of patrons had come to the alehouse for refreshment and to see the unusual sow. Lloyd was more than pleased to show his prized possession and ushered his patrons into the sty. Without bothering to look inside the pen himself, he turned to his audience and proudly boasted, "Now there's a sow for you! Has anyone ever seen anything like that?"

Seeing the drunken woman lying in such a state, some of the gapers thought that this was actually what Lloyd had brought them in to see and replied that it was the drunkennest sow they had ever seen. From that time on the woman was ever called David's Sow, and from that sobriquet the expression came into common use.

drunk as the devil: fourteenth century

drunk as a dog

drunk as a drum: seventeenth century. Today more likely to appear as "tight as a drum."

drunk as an emperor: late seventeenth century

drunk as a fiddler: early seventeenth century. During the Middle Ages when fiddlers played at fairs, parties or bride-ales, they were paid in ale instead of money. Since this was all they got, many consumed capaciously. A drunken fiddler is more than noticeable and *drunk as a fiddler* became a common expression with variants such as *drunk as a Plymouth fiddler, drunk as a Gosport fiddler.*

drunk as a fiddler's bitch

drunk as a fiddler's whore

drunk as a fish: early eighteenth century

drunk as Floey: corrupton of Chloe to Floey

drunk as a fly

drunk as a fowl

drunk as a hog: seventeenth century

drunk as a hoot owl

drunk as a king

drunk as a lion: seventeenth century

drunk as a log

drunk as a loon: nineteenth century

drunk as a lord: seventeenth century. From the late eighteenth century the custom engaged in by the nobility of drinking to excess to prove one's virility. Nothing has changed but the nobility.

drunk as a monkey

drunk as a mouse: early fourteenth century, "Dornke is as a mous" (Chaucer, "The Knight's Tale," 1261).

drunk as muck: late nineteenth century

drunk as a newt

drunk as a nurse at a christening

drunk as an owl: eighteenth century

drunk as a pig: eighteenth century

drunk as a piss ant

drunk as a poet

drunk as a Polony: corruption of Pole. The Polish were once considered heavy drinkers.

drunk as a pope: fourteenth century. A reference to Pope Benedict XII (1334-1342) who indulged copiously and conspicuously.

drunk as a porter: seventeenth century

drunk as a rat: sixteenth century

drunk as a rolling fart

drunk as a sailor

drunk as a skunk: twentieth century

drunk as soot: late nineteenth century

drunk as a sow: *See* drunk as David's Sow. The pig is also one of the few animals that will voluntarily drink large amounts of alcohol. This has led to its being used as an "animal model" in scientific studies of alcoholism. Although this particular "drunk as. . ." is probably a corruption of David's sow," the predilection of pigs for alcohol may have inspired this proverbial comparison. (*See* drunk as a hog, . . . pig, . . . swine.)

drunk as a swine: fifteenth century

drunk as a tapster

drunk as a tick

drunk as a tinker: early eighteenth century

drunk as a wheelbarrow: seventeenth century

Drunk is no longer used only in its specific sense. It has evolved as a metaphor for "excited," "overwhelmed," "elated," "overconfident," and a whole host of words which generally imply a cerebral intoxication not caused by alcohol but bearing a strong relationship to an alcohol-induced condition. Some people become "drunk with power." Others, like the "Iranians are blind drunk with hatred of the U.S." (*U.S. News & World Report,* 28 January 1980, 32).

If you're inclined to overeating, and you don't like to be called a "foodaholic" you may prefer to be known, along with a writer for *Cosmopolitan* (March 1960, 70), as a "food drunk." Or, if you're dieting and really believe you'll lose those ten pounds overnight, you may be "drunk with hope" like Dashiel Hammett's Gabrielle Legget: "Go away," she cried. "Don't give me any more assurances, any more of your promises, please. I can't stand any more tonight. I'm drunk on them now."

Boxers who have taken too many blows to the head may become "punch drunk" as a result of a cerebral concussion. Confused, unsteady on their feet, hands shaking uncontrollably, speech slurred, they seem groggy, like someone who has had the proverbial "one too many." *Punch drunk* first appeared in print in 1918 in the *Saturday*

Evening Post and was shortened to *punchy* in the 1930s. Around the same time, punch-drunk ex-fighters became *punchies,* not from throwing unches but from receiving one "too many."

There's no medical reason for it, but punch drunk seems to be contagious. At least that's the impression one might get from an article in *New Republic* (28 January 1985, 15) whose title ran: "Punch-drunk writers: the lost romance of boxing." Two years earlier (21 February 1983) *New Republic* said, "Reporters [were] punch-drunk with all the statistics they got from the White House last week." There was no comment on the condition of the White House sources.

Drunkard

A heavy drinker is in the eye of the beholder; drunkards and alcoholics are eyesores. A heavy drinker is someone who drinks more than you but doesn't necessarily get drunk. A drunkard is someone who chooses to drink too much too often and habitually gets drunk. A drunkard differs from an alcoholic in voluntarily drinking himself into oblivion, whereas an alcoholic doesn't seem able to keep himself from drinking.

Heavy drinkers are known as:

after-dinner men	brandy sunters
afternoon men	gin heads
barley caps	glow worms
bezzlers	histers
blossom noses	hooch histers
booze heisters	jake hounds
booze histers	juicers
booze kings	lap dogs
booze shunters	liquor plugs
boozers	low-country soldiers

lushing men
men who know how the
    cards are dealt
relishers of all waters
rum heads
rum jockeys
sipters

sound cards
sponges
sportsmen for liquor
stiff blades
true blues
two-fisted drinkers
whales

Drunkards are:

admirals of the red
aleheads
ale-wisps
bacchants
bacchantes
bang-pitcher
barrel dossers
barrel house bums
beer barrels
beer slingers
belchers
belch-guts
bench whistlers
benders
bibbers
big drunks
bloats
bloaters
blokes
blots
blotters
blowbolls
booze fighters
booze guzzlers

booze hitters
borrachos
botas
bottle-a-day men
bottle crackers
bottle heisters
brandy faces
brewer's horses
bubbers
garglers
gulches
gusseys
guzzle guts
habituals
hoisters
hooch hounds
hounds
inebriants
inebriates
jakes
love pots
lushing coves
lushingtons
maltworms

mops
muddlers
mug blots
nazy nobs
oilers
peggers
pot wallopers
potleech
potmen
rob-pots
rowing men
rum bags
rum dumbs
rum pots
rum soaks
rum suckers
rummies
scowrers
scrambled eggs
sewer pipes
shakers
shickers
sinkers
slaves of the beast
slubbers
slushers
shorters
soaks
soakers
sod
sodden bums
sons of Bacchus

sops
sots
souses
speck bums
stale drunks
stew bums
stewed fruit
stewies
stiffs
stills
suckers
suck-spiggots
swell heads
swiggers
swill-bellies
swill-pots
swipers
swizzle guts
swizzle nicks
tanks
taverners
tipplers
toasts
toast-and-butter men
topers
tosspots
wassailers
wetsters
whiskey bottles
winos
wino good-for-nothings

Alcoholics are known as:

alchys
alkis
alkys
alcoholists
alki (alky) stiffs
barrel stiffs
beer-jerkers
bingo boys
bingo morts
black pots
booze artists
booze hounds
boozegobs
boozers
bottle babies
bottle men
bottle suckers
Bowery bums
budgers
bum-boozers
gas hounds
gin bottlemen
grog hounds
guzzlers

helpless drunks
hold-out artists
homeguards
hootchers
jick heads
John alcoholics
jolly noses
juggers
juice heads
lappers
lappy culls
large heads
leaners
liquor heads
low bottom drunks
lushers
lusheys
martini alcoholics
nazy coves
oenophilists
oil heads
old soaks
pigeons
problem drinkers

(*See also* Amethyst.)

Dutch courage

In the seventeenth century, England and Hollard were rivals. It was
an era of expansionism and colonialism, and both countries wanted
their share of the world, and more. Both had large navies on which
they relied to protect their interests abroad. When the two countries
claimed the same territories, fighting was inevitable. In 1624, the
Dutch massacred the English at Ambonia in the East Indies. England
was not yet as powerful as she would soon become and was unable
to retaliate. To make matters worse, in 1652 a Dutch ship sailed
through the English Channel with a broom as its masthead, sym-
bolizing that Holland had "swept the seas." England seemed helpless.

Feelings against the Dutch were naturally venomous in England
and a new vocabulary was born using "Dutch" as a modifier meaning "inferior," "negative," or "bad." Some of these terms like *Dutch
cheese,* "a bald-headed person," *Dutch gold,* "worthless metal," and
Dutch window, "a prostitute," are no longer heard.

Others like *Dutch courage* are still with us, but have nothing to
do with the erstwhile conflict which ended in 1677 when William III,
the Dutch king, married Mary, princess of England. In 1689 William
became king of England, burying for good the old animosity between
the two countries. But Holland had another historic rival—France—
and one of the first things William did after becoming king of
England was to place heavy duties on French wines and liquors to
discourage their importation. At the same time Parliament passed
laws to encourage distillation, and the English soon began making
gin, an art acquired from the Dutch who had invented it in the
seventeenth century. So much was produced that gin consumption
leaped from about a half million gallons to about 18 million within
twenty years.

Dutch courage, meaning courage induced by alcohol, has nothing to do with the blood feud between the two countries, since the
expression did not appear until the beginning of the nineteenth
century. Instead, it arose in the aftermath of laws passed to curtail

gin-making, which had caused what many called a "gin epidemic." Having grown to like the taste of gin, a name they anglicized from its original appellation, "geneva," Britons refused to give it up without a fight. Mobs roamed the streets, and violence against authority was commonplace, inspired by a false courage brought on by gin— hence Dutch courage.

Embezzle

"Who will audit the auditors?" asked *Newsweek* magazine (13 March 1984) in an article describing the misfortunes of Arthur Andersen and Co., one of the country's most highly rated accounting firms. The company, it seems, became careless in auditing the ledgers of more than one of its clients and failed to detect several frauds. When these clients discovered the frauds on their own, they sued the accounting firm for malpractice. One more nail was driven into the firm's coffin, said *Newsweek,* when Andersen's auditors failed to discover a clear case of embezzlement.

Years ago newspapers and newsmagazines regularly printed stories about a bank teller or manager who embezzled hundreds of thousands of dollars. Today embezzlement is at an all time high, but tellers or managers are no longer the principal culprits. In fact it is very unusual to hear about a teller or manager making off with a bank's holdings. Today's embezzler more often than not is a young white male in his twenties or thirties sitting hunched in front of computer keyboard.

The computer is an admirable weapon for stealing from banks. Instead of pointing a gun at someone, a computer thief simply punches a few codes into the computer and tells it to remove perhaps a penny from each of the bank's accounts and deposit them into another account. There's no physical violence, no need to "case the joint," plan a get-a-way at break-neck speed; no need to have an accomplice who might behave irrationally. Nor does the computer thief have to get his hands dirty taking the money out of a drawer.

And then there's the intellectual challenge of it all.

Best of all, if he gets caught, the computer thief does not go to a prison for hard-core criminals but to a minimum security jail for the white-collar desperado, where he can compare notes with prisoners of a similar intellectual bent.

Many computer embezzlements are not even prosecuted, especially when they involve very large sums of money. For one thing, the institution that has been robbed prefers to keep its vulnerability secret so investors won't think their interests are in jeopardy. For another, on the principle that "it takes a thief to catch a thief," the same institutions often hire the computer embezzler as a security agent to make sure that other employees don't get the same idea.

Whether they work with computers or are bookkeepers in small businesses, embezzlers are usually very sober people, not at all the boozing type. Yet if you remove the "em" in "embezzle" you are left with a word that means just that. In medieval days, one didn't go "boozing," but "bezzling." *To bezzle* meant to drink a lot, and a *bezzler* was a drunkard.

Bezzle comes from the Latin *imbecillare,* "to weaken," an "imbecile" being someone whose intellect is weakened. A *bezzler* is a drunkard whose reason is weakened by alcohol. An *embezzler* is someone who steals from an organization thereby weakening it financially.

Eye-opener

An *eye-opener* is something surprising or unusually enlightening—it literally causes the eyes to open wide. This uniquely American word was first used around 1818 to refer to a drink of whiskey taken soon after awakening. Like "a hair of the dog that bit you," the intent is to restore life by ingesting some of what almost ended it the night before.

The first time I was asked if I wanted an eye-opener was in Brennan's, the famous restaurant in New Orleans. It was 9:00 A.M., and the place was filled with sober-looking academic types like myself. Nevertheless, the waiter asked at each table whether anyone cared for an eye-opener. When he came to my table I tried to be nonchalant and looked at my wife as if she might. "No, thank you," she said. "No, thank you," I replied, trying my best to seem urbane enough that the answer might have gone either way.

Flap-dragon

Popular during the late Middle Ages, *flap-dragon* is rarely heard today. It means a trifle, something inconsequential, of no importance. It comes from a drinking game in which a small combustible material, called a flap-dragon, was ignited at one end and floated in a glass of wine. Those who could drink the wine without getting burned were considered adept drinkers. In Shakespeare's *Love's Labour's Lost* (5.1.45) Costard says to Most, "Thou art easier swallow'd than a flap-dragon."

Free lunch

Speaking of the United States Supreme Court's 1984 ruling concerning aid to college students who refuse to register for military service, *Newsweek* (16 July 1984, 57) said, "the court upheld the no-free-lunch theory."

Free lunch means "something for nothing," a "handout," "welfare," "getting something without working for it," or "with no strings attached." The expression (raised to a "theory" by *Newsweek*) originated in Chicago in the 1870s when saloon operator Joe Mackin thought up a new idea for attracting customers to his bar. With every drink sold Mackin gave the customer a free hot oyster. The idea of the free lunch caught on, and soon everyone else in Chicago was offering some kind of free food with the drinks they sold.

The free lunch was not exactly free. Dead-beats were usually given a polite but firm warning that they were expected to buy drinks if they wanted to eat. Those not heeding the warning often got the "bum's rush" out the door.

Some hotels put out a spectacular table of treats. The Waldorf in its early days spent more than $7,500 a year on "free lunches" at its bar, but the wine and liquor consumed by patrons with these meals more than made up the cost.

The "free lunch" has gone the way of the horse-and-buggy and the slide rule. Instead of sumptuous sandwiches piled high with ham or turkey, the only thing one is likely to get free at a bar these days is a bowl of salty peanuts. The "free lunch" is no more. The Supreme Court outlawed it.

Fusty

On 3 July 1985 the *Wall Street Journal* carried a story about how the Wimbledon tennis match was saved from debacle by an infusion of cash. "Crass cash props up fusty tourney," was how the business newspaper put it. This was probably the first, and possibly the last, time *fusty* will appear in the *WSJ.*

Fusty has seen better days since its first appearance in the four-teenth century when it meant something damp or mouldy. In Samuel Pepys's day (seventeenth century) *fusty* was used to describe someone peevish or in bad temper: "At noon home to dinner," writes the diarist," where my wife still in a melancholy, fusty humour. . . ." (*Diary,* 18 June 1668).

Fusty comes from the Old French word *fuste,* meaning "smelling or tasting of the [wine] cask." Eventually it acquired the sense of "old-fashioned" or "conservative," like the Wimbledon tourney.

Good wine needs no bush.

This expression dates back to the early Middle Ages.

In those days most people drank ale, and brewing was an art. Although anyone could be a brewer, ale could be sold legally only after certification by the local ale taster, or aleconner. This was necessary because many brewers, bypassing accepted methods, poured sugar into their brews.

The first phase of certification involved tasting. An ale had to taste good or it would not earn the aleconner's approval. Next came quality inspection. No instrument was available to the aleconner to determine whether the sugar in a brew was natural or adulterated, so he relied on the seat of his pants! Putting on a pair of leather breeches, he poured some ale onto a table and sat in it. A few minutes later he got up. If his rear stuck to the table, it meant that sugar had been added to the brew. For that infraction the aleconner promptly fined the tavern keeper and had his ale spilt into the street.

Because there were so many taverns, a way had to be invented to let the aleconner know his services were needed. The message was borne by an "alestake," or pole placed in a hole near the roof of the tavern. Attached to the end of this pole, like a flag, was a branch or bush of ivy leaves, ivy being the plant sacred to Bacchus, the Greek god of wine. Since the brewer knew that the aleconner would undoubtedly discover ale that had been illegally adulterated, placing "the bush" outside meant his ale was good.

The expression *good wine needs no bush* literally meant that a customer did not have to see "the bush" to know whether a brewer's ale (and later, wine) were good. Subsequently it came to mean that quality needs no official stamp of approval. If something is good, customers will tell their friends, and they in turn will tell others. In even broader terms it carries the idea expressed in the modern proverb: "Virtue is its own reward." A good product or a good deed does not have to be advertised or embellished in any way.

Winemakers in Burgenland, an eastern part of Austria, were

well aware of this concept. For years they had been producing a sweet dessert wine especially liked by German tourists, one for which the Germans were willing to pay a good price.

But the winemakers of Burgenland were able to produce only a relatively small amount of the wine each year. Finally, greed got the better of some, and they tried a little alchemy. To one of their cheap, light, dry wines they added sugar and a thickening agent, diethylene glycol, the stuff put in car radiators each winter.

When the scandal broke in 1985, Austrian wines were yanked from shelves around the world, and the Austrian wine industry as a whole suffered a major setback. Then anti-freeze was also found in German and Italian wines, and a worldwide search was begun for tainted wines. In Italy, governmental action was swift. Eight Sicilian winemakers were fined 77 million lira and given one-to-four-year prison terms for adding sugar and food coloring to their product.

Punishments for adulterating alcohol have obviously become more severe than in the days of the aleconner.

Groggy

When a British sailor went to sea in bygone days, he had little to look forward to. Life was hard, boring, and dangerous. If wounded in a naval battle, he would probably die for lack of adequate medical attention. If lucky enough not to be in a fight at sea, he might be swept overboard during a storm. The one positive thing he could look forward to was a daily half pint of rum, usually doled out at noon. Most sailors drank it in one gulp as soon as it was poured.

The daily rum ration had become so much a part of naval tradition that few captains would have dared to do away with it, despite its obvious effects on coordination and efficiency. But Edward Vernon (1684-1757) was no ordinary captain. A tough and determined seadog, Vernon expected his men to be equally dedicated and tough. His men respected and feared him, calling him "Old

Grog" because he always appeared on deck during rough weather in a grogram cloak, made from a coarse fabric of silk and wool.

In the summer of 1740, "Old Grog" decided that the daily rum ration was impairing his crew's abilities, so he ordered the ship's rum stock to be diluted with two parts water to one part rum. Moreover, instead of each seaman being given his ration all at once, Vernon ordered it divided in two, the second to be dispensed no earlier than six hours after the first. Not long after he implemented these new rules, "Old Grog's" crew defeated a much superior Spanish naval force at the battle of Carthagena in 1741. For this victory Edward Vernon was promoted to admiral. When other captains in the British navy heard about Vernon's victory, they attributed it to the diluted rum ration. As a result watered-down rum was soon adopted throughout the navy and was called "grog" by less-than-happy British seamen.

Weaker though it might have been compared to its undiluted predecessor, grog still packed a pretty hefty wallop, one that made the novice unsteady on his feet, wobbly, and confused. By 1770, those unfortunate enough to experience this condition were called *groggy*.

Grog soon became a generic term for any kind of liquor, and places where grog was sold became known as *grog shops* or *groceries*.

Grog was not the only thing named after Vernon. The admiral was also a good friend of George Washington's half-brother Laurence, who had served under him. It was out of Laurence's fondness and respect for him that the first president's estate, Mount Vernon, was so named.

Hangover

Time magazine (26 November 1984, 86) described as a financial hangover the beating New Orleans suffered from hosting the 1984 World's Fair.

Long accustomed to the annual rollicking roistering of Mardi Gras and the more frequent revels of Bourbon street night-life, the city fathers expected the French Quarter's hotels, bars, restaurants, and souvenir shops to attract tourist dollars like Richmond attracted Grant. Alas, the rest of the country was not in the mood to spend the money to travel to the Bayou City or to pay $15 per day for admission. Its coffers parched, the fair sent up the white flag and filed for bankruptcy five days before the scheduled closing day.

The dull, throbbing fiscal headache; the dry, caked mouth unable to ask "how deep" the debacle; the fetid breath that finally forces the words out; the incessant ringing, a tolling in the ears instead of in cash registers; the queasy stomach unable to keep the answer down once it penetrated beyond the ringing; the nausea, the wooziness, the dry heaves . . . this was the city's financial *hangover.*

Many cures have been recommended for reducing the misery of the "morning after": from the proverbial "hair of the dog that bit you," first penned in 1546 by Thomas Heywood ("I praie the leat me and my felowe haue A heare of the dog that bote us last nyght") to Jeeves's famous concoction.

Robert Benchley knew better. "There is no cure for the hangover, save death," said Benchley. Fortunately he was exaggerating a bit. Hangovers do go away eventually. Only to arise phoenix-like when the next World's Fair arrives? Or to make their way into magazine or newspaper headlines. Here are some examples of the ubiquitous *hangover:*

Emotional hangover: growing up with an alcoholic parent. (*McCall's* October 1984, 161)

Ashland Oil: trying to cope with a diversification hangover and a lingering scandal. (*Business Week,* 7 November 1983, 132)

Cleaning up a hygienic hangover [lysol]. (*Macleans,* 1 August 1983, 34)

Recession's harsh hangover. (*Newsweek*, 16 May 1983, 69)

The cure for a thirty-year hangover: the entitlement program. (*Vital Speeches*, 15 December 1982, 154)

A birthday party hangover. [corruption in Boston politics]. (*Time*, 3 January 1983, 49)

Mexico's petroleum hangover [economic problems]. (*Time*, 29 March 1982, 50)

Canada: an oil hangover for Hiram Walker. (*Business Week*, 22 February 1982, 50)

Hangover from West Germany's "miracle." (*U.S. News & World Report*, 19 January 1981, 32)

Three Mile Island hangover: treat the basic problem, not the symptoms. (*Dun's Review*, July 1980, 96)

Hangover on job restrictions [*Transit Authority* v. *Beazer*]. (*Monthly Labor Review*, May 1979, 53)

A Hearst trial hangover? Patty thinks F. Lee Bailey had one and blew her case; now he's blown his stack. (*People*, 4 September 1978, 24)

Hangover from a demonstration; weekend peace demonstrations in Washington, D.C. (*America*, 4 November 1967, 495)

Scourge of Hangover Alley; speed festival at Nassau. (*Sports Illustrated*, 14 December 1964, 68).

(*See also* Butler.)

High jinks

In 1968, Detroit hurler Denny McLain won 31 games, the first 30-

game winner since 1934. He went on to win the Cy Young Award, and his future seemed secure.

McLain was a colorful baseball character who used to joke about his betting exploits, claiming he was the only gambler with an interest in a betting shop that lost money. Anyone else would have been censured, but as *Time* magazine (1 April 1985, 86) noted, "Betting [among sports people] had long since been classified as high jinks," and such transgressions were overlooked.

McLain's arm gave out soon after his amazing 31-game season and his baseball career ended. After he left baseball, his life fell apart. Everything he tried failed, and he wound up in a Florida jail accused of racketeering, extortion, and cocaine possession. This was no longer "high jinks."

Years ago, before kids started carrying knives, chains or guns, and mayhem was a word so rare we had to look it up in the dictionary, any trouble teenagers got into was attributed to youthful high jinks rather than to malevolence. Like McLain, *high jinks* has seen better days.

High jinks was originally a drinking game played in Scottish pubs in the eighteenth century, not a term for mischief. The game involved a group of players seated around a table, glasses filled to the brim with ale or beer. Each player chose a number from two to twelve. To start, a player cried out "high jinks," and threw dice onto the table. The number that came up indicated which of the players was to empty his glass. His glass was then refilled, and it became his turn to cry out "high jinks" and throw the dice. As the night grew longer, the players became progressively more drunk. The winner was the one who could still remember to say "high jinks." To make the game more interesting, some players put a little money in the middle of the table, and the person whose number was called kept it. The more a player could drink, the longer he could stay in the game, and the more he could win. So each player tried to drink his opponents *under* the table to keep what was *on top*.

As the game gained popularity, "high jinks" became synonymous with fun that might attract mild social disapproval. Danny McLain's kind of fun went beyond high jinks to a no-win game called felony arrest.

Hobnob

With more than two years to go (at this writing) before the race for the 1988 presidential nomination officially starts, Republican Party hopefuls are already out of the starting box. The acknowledged leaders thus far are Vice President George Bush and New York Congressman Jack Kemp. No one has actually declared as a candidate yet, but no one is passing up an opportunity to score points. So when New Hampshire Republicans invited prospective candidates to a no-speeches-allowed fund-raiser, some of them showed up anyway. One was Jack Kemp who, *Newsweek* (2 December 1985, 54) said, hustled "to Manchester by car, plane, and helicopter to hobnob with GOP activists."

In the days of Frances Grose, whose slang dictionary of 1785 was the first of its kind, a request to *hob or nob* was an invitation to have a glass of beer. The person to whom the offer was made had the choice of having it warm or cold. Warm beer was called hob because in winter, beer was sometimes warmed on a grate called the hob, located in the corner of a large chimney. Alternatively, cold beer, or rather beer served at room temperature, was set on a small table called a nob. The question, "hob or nob?" thus meant "warm or cold beer?"

Acceptance of the invitation would result in familiarity and a certain intimacy among those drinking together. By extension, *hob or nob,* later shortened to *hobnob,* meant familiarity and intimacy even when there was no drinking.

Hocus pocus

Hocus pocus is an expression synonymous with amateur legerdemain. To distract an audience, a magician utters an unintelligible command which conjures in the mind a mysterious summoning of spirits to help accomplish the astounding feats to be performed.

And "spirits" are exactly what is referred to when the magician says those arcane words, for *hocus* means to induce stupefaction by drugging someone's wine or liquor. Someone who has been "hocused" has been slipped a "Mickey Finn." "What do you mean by hocussing brandy and water?" asks Dickens's Pickwick. "Puttin' laund'num in it," replied Sam.

When the magician says "hocus pocus," the mind is being metaphorically stupefied for the purpose of tricking the senses.

Honeymoon

"Honeymoon is over for Mulroney government," said the *New York Times* (9 October 1985, N13). It seems that Canada's Prime Minister Brian Mulroney had in the eyes of the Canadian electorate begun to lose some of his charm. The smiling face that had posed with U.S. President Ronald Reagan just a short summer before had turned grim with the Canadian autumn.

Politicians seem inexorably destined to have their honeymoons short lived. In December of 1984, the *Wall Street Journal* (14 December, 1) reflected that "[Elizabeth] Dole's honeymoon as transportation secretary may be ending." A few months earlier it had observed that the newly appointed head of the Environmental Protection Agency, William Ruckelshaus, was being "criticized by all sides as honeymoon at EPA nears end" (6 April 1984, 2.31). California's Governor George Deukmejian was not even permitted the usual accord: "Deukmejian off to a turbulent start," observed the *Los Angeles Times* (16 January 1983, 1.3); "state budget crisis does away with traditional honeymoon."

Political honeymoons are those brief post-election interludes when elected officials have not yet upset anyone. This is because they have done nothing as yet. Inevitably they will do something, and inevitably someone won't like it. And that will be the end of the honeymoon.

A honeymoon is a holiday. For newlyweds it is a time to get to know one another while having a good time. No dishes to wash, no bills to pay, no phones to answer, no alarm clock to pound into submission. It's a time of affection and passion. But why call it a honeymoon?

The modern honeymoon carries on a tradition begun in Roman times. During the heyday of the Empire three boys accompanied the bride during the marriage ceremony—one to carry a torch, since all marriages took place at night, and the other two to support the bride. After the marriage, the bride was brought to her new home and given a special drink made with honey, poppy seeds and milk:

> Let poppy bruised and snow-white milk be dressed
> With liquid honey from the cells expressed,
> When Venus first was brought to Vulcan's side
> Of this she drank and thus became a bride.
>
> (Ovid, *Fasti,* 4.151).

This basic ceremony was kept in tact for centuries with minor variations. In England during the reign of King Henry VII, two bridegrooms walked with the bride, while the third carried a cup of silver or gold instead of a torch. When the bride was brought to her new home, she drank a cup of honey wine. Later, the honey wine was drunk in the church immediately after the priest's blessing. After the bride had drunk, the groom and everyone else would also drink. Honey wine drunk on this occasion was sometimes called "a knitting cup."

The reason for this custom was the almost universal belief that honey was an aphrodisiac. An Arabic poem, for instance, relates that "Abou al-Heidja has deflowered in one night, / Once eighty virgins, and he did not eat or drink between, / Because he'd surfeited himself first with chick-peas, / And had drunk camel's milk with honey mixed." Attila the Hun, known to history as "the scourge of God," was a devout believer in honey's aphrodisiac properties. Too much so. On his wedding night he drank so much honey wine that he died of alcohol poisoning.

Honeymoon is literally "30 days of honey" and means 30 days of drinking honey wine. Beginning on their wedding day and every day after that for the first month of their marriage, the newlyweds drank honey wine. This was to keep their ardor high and to increase their chances of pregnancy. After that first month, the marriage needed more than honey:

> When a couple are newly-married, the first month is
> honey-moon or smick-smack;
> The second is hither and thither: The third is thwick thwack:
> The fourth, the Devil take them that brought thee
> and I together.

Inebriate, intoxicate

Unlike *drunk, inebriated* conveys a certain degree of urbanity. You can get away with being "inebriated" in some circles, but if you're "drunk," you're too common to associate with.

Though both *drunk* and *inebriated* mean the same thing, one is pejorative, the other descriptive. You can be "drunk as a pig" or "drunk as a skunk" but never inebriated like one. It just doesn't fit. When you're inebriated you're uplifted; your spirits are aloft; you have risen above the crowd, not fallen in a stupor at its feet.

Inebriated comes directly from Latin *ebrius,* "drunk" and *bria,* "cup." Someone who is *in his cups,* an expression over 200 years old, is inebriated.

Intoxicated also means drunk but is less vulgar. This is the way with polysyllabic words. They have a way of softening the blow. *Drunk* is a knock-down, no-nonsense word. *Intoxicated* is more refined. It also has a more colorful history, and its roots make it the more treacherous of the two.

Intoxicated comes from Greek *toxon,* "a bow." *Toxikon* was the Greek word for "arrow poison," or "arrow dipped in poison." Latin adopted the word modifying it to *intoxicare,* "to poison." In English, the word became *intoxicate* and retained its meaning in a figurative rather than a literal sense. The mind of someone who is intoxicated is temporarily poisoned or excited beyond control. Still, *intoxication* has retained its original meaning, for example when physicians talk about acute alcoholic intoxication, which means alcohol poisoning—or drinking so much at one time that the vital centers of the brain almost stop working, as if poisoned.

Poison can also mean *liquor* as in "name your poison." Always hard liquor, mind you. Never wine or beer. Can you imagine a sommelier asking his patrons if they would care to "name their poison"? It's just not done. If you're being asked to name you're poison, you're probably the bad guy in a western movie.

Intoxicated has more in common with *drunk* than does *inebriated.* Just as you can be "drunk with power," you can be "intoxicated by . . . power" (*New York Times,* 1 September 1982, N22), or you can be "intoxicated with romance" (*Time,* 4 June 1973, 69). Rarely is anyone these days ever inebriated with anything but booze.

The Katzenjammer Kids

People read newspapers to find out what is happening in the world and in their own community. After the depressing litany of maimings, muggings, local wars, business failures and unemployment figures, many finally turn to the comic strips for escape.

Long before radio and television, comic strips were among the most popular opiates for the masses. The first of these mass-cultural palliatives appeared in the United States in 1897. Published in the *New York Journal,* it was called "The Katzenjammer Kids."

The Katzenjammer kids were two German urchins, Hans and Fritz. Mischief was their pablum and havoc their milk. Despite inevitable and innumerable punishments doled out for their misdeeds, the turmoil continued day after day.

Then came World War I. Germany was the enemy and anything German was anathema, a German surname most of all. England's Lord Brattenborough became "Mountbatten" and the "Katzenjammer Kids" became "The Shenanigan Kids." After the war, when the venom against Germans dissipated, the name reverted to "The Katzenjammer Kids" again. The slapstick and mayhem continued to delight kids and adults alike until 1968 when the Kids finally disappeared, done in by time, not war.

Why did cartoonist Rudolph Dirks call his brats Katzenjammer? It was actually a joke. In German *katzenjammer* literally means "yowling of cats." Figuratively, it is German slang for a hangover. The idea behind the German is "confusion, uproar, yowling, disorder"—in short, anarchism—the kind of behavior and aftermath associated with heavy drinking.

Just as many people who have drunk too much are often unable to control their impulses, the Katzenjammer Kids were unrestrained in their play. The chaos they provoked was like the anarchy of a mind stripped by alcohol of its inhibitions. The price the kids paid for their mischief was a spanking; the retribution for too much drinking is a head-splitting hangover.

When Dirks named his strip, few Americans appreciated the allusion. Knowing that *katzenjammer* means "hangover," it is much less surprising, given the reputation of the Irish for hard drinking, that during the war Dirks gave them an Irish surname.

Leave some for manners.

Most parents are always after their children to finish eating what is on their plates. The spectre of children starving in China was supposed to convince even the fussiest eater to lick his platter clean. Yet in polite society it was once considered very unrefined to eat everything placed before one at a dinner party. Instead, the accepted practice was to "leave some for manners"—leave food on the plate so as not to appear hungry, something only a servant or common man would admit to.

Originally the expression applied only to the wine glass and the wine bottle. The custom appears to have started with King Henry I, who issued a standing order for a carafe of wine to be put in his bedroom every night. Since Henry was one of England's most abstemious kings, he rarely drank any of it himself. Instead, his servants consumed it as a nightcap. One evening Henry felt like a nightcap himself, but there was nothing left for him.

The custom of putting a carafe of wine in the monarch's bedroom was still practiced during Queen Victoria's reign, although she was even more abstemious than Henry. When her son Edward VII became king and learned that for nearly the entire 75-plus years of his mother's reign the servants had been drinking the royal wine, he put an end to the custom. Incidentally, unlike his mother, Edward was quite fond of drinking.

At loggerheads

"After battling for a year—in and out of court—the governing board of the Friends of the Earth and the group's founder, David Brower, are still at loggerheads," reported *Newsweek* on 27 January 1986. Being "at loggerheads" has nothing to do with logging or trees. Generally it refers to a negotiation that has reached an impasse. In this instance, the factions were arguing about closing the San Francisco office and moving the organization's headquarters to Washington (Brower didn't want to, the board did).

Some etymologists trace the origins of *at loggerheads* to colonial days when one of the most popular drinks was called "flip." The best liked of these was "rum flip," a concoction said to have been invented by Benjamin Franklin at the Golden Key tavern in Boston immediately after the Tea Party. It was made with rum, beer, beaten eggs, cream and spices which were heated or mulled by plunging a red hot bar with a rounded tip into the tankard until the drink hissed and bubbled. The hot bar was called a "loggerhead." Since the colonists usually drank quite a bit, fighting and arguing were common in American taverns in colonial days. Those who quarreled in such settings were sometimes said to be "at loggerheads," a reference to the belligerence brought on by drinking too much of the most popular drink of the day, Franklin's loggerhead-heated potion.

Another explanation is that the term comes from the days of the galleons. An essential piece of nautical equipment in those days was the *loggerhead,* a long iron ladle used to pour molten iron. When ships went to battle, opposing sailors boiled hot tar or oil and used loggerheads to burn one another. Being *at loggerheads* meant being in a "hot" fight. Now it means being in a heated argument.

Limey

Every school child knows that the British are called limeys because British seamen ate limes to ward off scurvy during their long ocean voyages.

Scurvy was once the bane of all sailors. During Queen Elizabeth I's reign, more than 20,000 British seamen died of it. A vitamin C deficiency disease, scurvy causes the gums to soften and the teeth to fall out; legs and arms swell, and death eventually follows. In 1753, Dr. James Lind had discovered that lemon juice could prevent scurvy, and he tried to convince the admiralty to give sailors lemon juice to prevent the disease. But for forty years no one paid any attention. One of the reasons Lind's discovery was never appreciated is that the vitamin C in fruit juice is quickly broken down by heat unless it can be preserved in some way. It was left to another scientist to show that all that was necessary to preserve the vital anti-scurvy element in lemon juice was to mix lemon juice with alcohol.

Lime juice was eventually substituted for lemon juice, and in the Caribbean it was mixed with rum. Australian and American sailors called their British counterparts "limejuicers," an expression later shortened to "limeys." But many were convinced it was the pre-servative that was responsible for the sailors' new-found health, and British seamen could just as well have been called "rummies" as "limeys."

Loving cup, or grace cup

A loving cup is a large trophy given to the winner of some contest. Initially, it was a silver bowl with two handles. There are at least three stories about how it came to be, none of which has to do with contests.

In the first story the loving cup was fashioned as a ploy by a noblewoman in Scotland to keep her guests from leaving her banquet table before grace was said. Usually the lords ate and ran. To keep them put, the lady had her craftsmen create a large cup. Just before her guests were about to leave, she had her servants fill it with the best wine from her cellars, allowing each guest to choose a wine and to drink as much as he wished. The cup was passed around the table and everyone drank. The only catch was that the guests had to stay for the grace, since it was said before the wine was passed.

The second explanation is that loving cup was just another name for the wassail bowl, a bowl of ale carried from house to house during New Year festivities. This bowl was called by the monks *poculum caritatis,* Latin for "loving cup."

The third explanation goes back to the tenth century, following the Danish invasion of England. One of the ways the conquerors imposed their dominion over the conquered was to forbid any Englishman to drink without permission in front of a Dane. Those who broke the law could be killed immediately for such an affront. The only exception was if a Dane stood at his side and pledged to defend him against other Danes. When the Danes ceased to control England, the practice disappeared, but the idea of "defending" a drinker was carried on at English banquets.

At such festivities, two men would stand, one to drink out of a large silver bowl with two handles, the other to symbolically protect the drinker as had the Danish patron in the past. After the first man drank, he wiped the cup with a napkin attached to one of the handles, passed it to the defender, and sat down. The defender then became the drinker, and the man next to him would rise and become the new defender, and so on around the table. In this way each man would take his turn as drinker and defender.

In England two men still stand when one rises to propose a toast, a carryover from the time of the Danish invasion. It is also from the Danish conquest of England and the protection provided by the conquerors to their favorites that we have the custom of awarding a bowl or loving cup to the winner or "conqueror" in a contest. The winner "defends" the title and keeps the cup as a symbol of his defense. (*See also* Wassail.)

Lush

A *lush* is an alcoholic. Before acquiring this specific sense, *lush* meant "to drink alcohol," or it was another term for strong beer. *Lush* made its appearance in the late 1700s, apparently bursting into English from nowhere. The *Oxford English Dictionary* merely says that it is slang and of obscure origin. Since this is so, several sources are possible. Among the more likely is derivation from a well-known

English brewer named Lushington, or from the "City of Lushing-ton," a London club located in Bow Street, where well-known actors of the day socialized. The third suggestion is that it is simply an extension of the meaning "full of juice." In many languages juice is slang for alcohol, and lush is just another way of saying juice. In Scotland, for example, whiskey is called "juice of the barley." The final possibility is that our word comes from German *loschen*, "to drink."

The English have a fondness for *lush*. Among the words they have coined from it are *lushery, lush crib, lush ken,* or *lush house* (all meaning a disreputable tavern); *lush, lushey, lushie, lushy, lusher, lushington, lushing cove,* and *lushing man* (all with the sense of drunkard); a *lush diver, lush toucher,* or *lush worker* (a thief) who waits for a *lush* to emerge *lushed,* or *lushed up* (in a drunken state) from a *lush crib* and then pulls off a *lush job* (robbery).

In the United States there is apparently a social hierarchy among the inhabitants of the nation's skid rows, with the lush at the top and the bum at the bottom: "The 'lushes,' the prestige group of alcoholics on Skid Road . . . maintain social distance from the other groups. . . .Most of the lushes usually drink wine and resort to nonbeverage alcohol only when desperate. They tend to be in better physical and mental condition than the winos and other characters, while their adherence to the mores of Skid Road society differentiates them from the bums" (Jackson and Connor, *Quarterly Journal of Studies on Alcohol 14* [1953]: 468).

Maudlin

Maudlin means overly sentimental to the point of tears.

Mary Magdalen is the biblical eponymous source for this word, often used in combination with drunk as in "maudlin drunk."

Mary Magdalen is first mentioned in the Bible as a "sinner," i.e., a prostitute who had seven devils driven from her body by Jesus

(Luke 8:2), but she is usually associated with the penitent prostitute who approaches Jesus while he is at supper with Simon the Pharisee (Luke 7:36-50). Mary has come to wash Jesus' feet with oil of myrrh. While doing so she cries and her tears fall on Jesus' feet. Immediately she wipes away her tears with her hair and kisses his feet. Jesus regards her actions as a sign of love and forgives her sins.

Mary is also described as being in tears as she stands by the empty tomb, distraught because she believed that Jesus' body had been stolen by grave robbers rather than having risen from the dead as promised. Jesus appears to her, and recognizing him she moves to touch him, but he commands her not to *("noli me tangere")*; instead, she is to tell his disciples that he has risen (John 20:14-18).

Mary began in the Middle Ages to be portrayed in Christian art as a penitent and was regularly so depicted during the Counter-Reformation in response to the Church's wish to encourage penance. Many of the great painters, Titian and Giotto among them, portrayed her in tears, her eyes looking upward, toward angels in heaven.

Mary's name was not connected with drunkenness until the sixteenth century. *Magdalene* went through several different spellings before becoming *maudlin*, but in some cases only the pronunciation changed. Magdalene college is called "Maudlin" college in England. But maudlin drunk is always spelled "maudlin." Thomas Nashe describes the condition as one in which someone "wil weepe for kindness in the mist of his ale and kisse you" (*Pierce Penilesse,* 207).

Moonraker

A moonraker is either a dim-wit or a smuggler. Though seemingly unrelated, these two meanings have a historical connection.

To evade the laws against importing whiskey into England, smugglers devised various ruses to escape detection. Occasionally they feigned stupidity to deceive their captors. One such case is the story of the Wiltshire moonrakers. These were smugglers from the village of Wiltshire in England. About to be caught by the king's agents, the smugglers sank their contraband whiskey in the village pond. Since they knew they were under suspicion, they took some long hay-rakes they had with them and started raking the water.

To the obvious question about what they were doing in the middle of the pond, the smugglers pointed to the moon's reflection in the water. "Raking the cheese from the water, your lordship," came the ingenuous reply. The king's agents went away laughing at these "moonrakers." No longer in any danger, the smugglers fished their whiskey from the pond and in turn laughed at the dim-witted soldiers who had believed such a preposterous story.

Moonshine

Moonshine is illegally manufactured whiskey, usually raw and potent. The term is very old and can be found in Grose's *A Classical Dictionary of the Vulgar Tongue* (1785), where two definitions are given. The first is "a matter or mouthful of moonshine; a trifle, nothing." The second, with its historical background, indicates that by the 1700s moonshine was already being used as a name for illegal whiskey: "The white brandy smuggled on the coasts of Kent and Sussex, and the gin in the north of Yorkshire." Grose does not say why it was called "moonshine," but the term possibly came from the fact that smuggling occurred at night when the moon was up.

Today, moonshine is produced by either the sour mash or sweet mash method. For making sweet mash moonshine—the more common of the two—corn is ground into meal and then placed in a large mash barrel called the still. The moonshiner then pours in scalding hot water, which acts to extract the starch, and stirs the mixture until it forms a thick mush. After the mixture has cooked, he adds ground rye, malt, and warm water, the malt acting to break down the starch and convert it to sugar. When the mash has been soaked and thoroughly stirred, yeast is added. The mixture is again stirred, and more malt, called the "cap" is put in. The beginning of fermentation is indicated by a bubbing activity called "snowballing." As the mash continues to ferment, carbon dioxide gas escapes, and a liquid containing a low percentage of alcohol rises to the top. This liquid is called "distillers' beer" or "still beer."

After fermentation is over (gauged by the smell, taste, and absence of bubbles), the mixture is heated. The alcohol vapor gathers in the "still cap," an area above the mash layer and below the top of the still. The vapor then moves through a tube, called the "worm," which passes into cold water. The cold water bath causes the vapor to condense, and the condensate is collected. The first condensate is called the "foreshot." This is followed by the "singlin's," or "low wines," indicated by the "bead" or bubbles. The first "bead" in the "singlin's" is called the "frog eyes" because these bubbles are bigger than the later bubbles. The middle portion of the distillate is the most prized. The last is called the "backin's," "tailin's," or "feints."

After the last of the distillate has been collected, the still is cleaned, and the first part, the "low wines," is redistilled, a process called "doublin'." This removes many impurities and raises the concentration of the alcohol. At the same time, some of the distillate from the middle of the run, the "high wines," is mixed in. The objective is to raise the concentration to about 50 percent (100 proof), a process called "drappin' the bead."

The sour mash procedure is similar to that for sweet mash, except that the moonshiner does not throw away the initial "spent" mash mixture; he collects this hot "slop" and uses it instead of hot water to scald the new mash, a process called "sloppin' back." In terms of taste or potency, there is little difference between moonshine made by the sweet or sour mash methods.

Martin drunk, St. Martin's goose, St. Martin's summer, gossamer

Like *maudlin drunk, martin drunk* is also an eponym drawn from the church. The source is St. Martin of Tours, patron saint of bartenders, reformed drunkards, drunkards with no thought of reform— and France. His feast day, 11 November, replaced the *vinalia,* an ancient Roman festival dedicated to Bacchus. The *vinalia* was celebrated to mark the time when wine reached its prime, an event heralded by more than a little tasting. Because of his association with this festival, St. Martin's name was attached to the condition brought on by too much drinking. *Martin drunk* means very drunk.

St. Martin was a Roman soldier who was converted to Christianity and subsequently refused to fight other Christians. He was made Bishop of Tours against his will around 370. The saint is a favorite subject in Christian art where he is often depicted in soldier's garb, mounted on horseback, cutting his military cloak in two with his sword to give half to a beggar. This portrayal stems from a legend surrounding St. Martin which tells of a naked beggar who asked him for charity. During the previous night, Jesus, wearing the same cloak, had appeared to Martin, an appearance which led to his conversion to Christianity.

St. Martin's name is also found in a number of other expressions. *St. Martin's goose* is our equivalent of a "dead duck." It came from another legend about the saint describing his annoyance by a goose, which the saint ordered to be killed and served for dinner. While feasting on the troublesome bird, the saint choked to death. To commemorate the event, a goose was sacrificed every St. Martin's day.

St. Martin's summer is the European equivalent of our "Indian summer" and was so named because weather on the saint's day is usually warm. Our word *gossamer,* plucked from obscurity by Cole Porter and immortalized as "gossamer wings," comes from the association of the goose legend with St. Martin's summer, which was also known as "goose summer." During this time, very delicate cobwebs float in the air; these used to be called "goose-summer webs" because geese were plentiful at that time of year. *Goose-summer* was later shortened to *gossamer.*

Mug, muggy

Years ago before they talked about barometric pressure, "fronts," the gulf stream, and a 30 percent chance of this or that, weather forecasters would say it was going to be sunny or it was going to rain, be foggy in the morning, or be muggy.

Weather forecasters are now more circumspect. They like to leave themselves an opening, so they say it's going to be "partly cloudy," or "partly sunny," or "there's a 75.3 percent chance of rain." It could be raining right outside their window, and they will say the humidity level is about 90 percent. That's because it isn't raining in their offices. For the rest of us the humidity is 100 percent—it's pouring, it's coming down in buckets, it's raining cats and dogs—but these guys won't admit it.

I prefer "sunny" or "cloudy" to "partly sunny" or "partly cloudy." And "muggy" says a lot more than "clear skies and 78 percent humidity."

Muggy means its hot and humid outside. There's no wind, and it's a good time to be lazy because you aren't going to get any work done out there anyway. It's the kind of day that will put you in the same state you would be in if you were tipsy, which muggy originally meant.

A cognate of muggy is *mughouse,* the name for an eighteenth century tavern. In the seventeenth century, mughouses were not just taverns but centers of political agitation. They appeared after George I became king of England. The Tories and the working class supported the king against the Whigs who were supported by the wealthy tradesmen. Mughouses were established in various areas of London as places where these tradesmen might meet and be ready, if need be, to challenge Tory-sponsored mobs.

Street fighting between the political factions was very common and finally culminated in the "mughouse riot" of 24 July 1716 which broke out on Fleet Street. The militia was called out to quell the disturbance and the mughouse where the riot started was demolished. Five ringleaders were arrested and later hanged.

Mug, a drinking vessel with a face on it, is another cognate of muggy. The reason mugs had funny and sometimes distorted faces was that in the eighteenth century patrons brought their own mugs to alehouses (subsequently called *mughouses)* and left them there. Since each mug was unique, everyone knew which mug was his. "Mug" meaning a face, comes from these old English drinking vessels, which are also the origin of the modern "mug-shot," a photograph of the face. By extension a "mug" is a person, usually someone not exactly handsome in appearance or behavior. Criminals got "mugged" when they had their pictures taken by the police. Now it's a victim who gets "mugged" (assaulted) by a "mugger" (robber).

Commenting on the spate of biographies dominating the best seller lists in 1985, *Detroit Free Press's* Book Editor, Bob McKelvey, called it the "Literary Age of the Non-Author" (29 December 1985, F1). The hallmark of this age, said McKelvey, is the author's picture prominently displayed on the cover and a second name, that of the "ghostwriter," or as McKelvey more generously calls him, the "collaborator," in small letters somewhere underneath. How can you tell if you're about to buy a "non-author" book? McKelvey answered by paraphrasing Marshall McLuhan. The first and best clue, he said, is if the "mug is the message."

Also related to muggy is the English drinking game, "muggle," better known today as "chug-a-lug." In the seventeenth century when muggle first became popular, it was played like this: The first player drank a pint of ale; the second, two pints; the third, three and so on until everyone in the group had drunk the number of drinks corresponding to his number. Then the first player started again where the last had left off.

Three hundred years later *muggles* was resurrected in New Orleans as a term for marijuana. In 1928 Louis Armstrong recorded "Muggles" and the same year the *Chicago Tribune* (1 July 1928, 12) warned "add a jot of 'muggles' to the artistic temperament of your journeyman musician and you've got discord." "Muggles" breathed its last in the 1950s, giving way to "grass" and "pot."

Neat

"Chicago," wrote columnist George Will in the 13 August 1984 edition of *Newsweek*, "takes life neat: no ice, no water" (p. 74). *Neat* is an old term for unadulterated wine or ale; it goes back to the late 1500s. For most people, however, neat means clean and tidy or refined and elegant. Both meanings have a common element.

Neat comes from Latin *nitidus,* "shiny," "bright," "clear." Something that's neat is free of "contamination," whether it is a room, a desk, clothes, or a drink.

Nelson's blood

Just before he died in 1805 aboard the *Victory* at the battle of Trafalgar, the famous British Admiral Horatio Nelson asked that he be buried not at sea but in his native England. In accord with his wishes, his officers put his body into a cask of rum to preserve it for burial until the ship returned to England.

During the return voyage, one of the marines appeared drunk on several occasions and eventually was threatened with flogging for breach of discipline unless he confessed the source of his illicit liquor. According to a newspaper account written in January 1806, the marine had "tapped the admiral"—he had bored a hole in the side of the cask containing Nelson's body and had used a pipe to suck out some of the "preservative," drinking "Nelson's spirit" (his blood) along with the rum spirits!

Grisly though the incident was, rum became known as *Nelson's blood* and *tapping the admiral* became another expression for drinking. While *Nelson's blood* never referred to anything other than rum, *tapping the admiral* was soon extended to any situation involving illegal entry.

Nip

In its May 1855 issue *Harper's Magazine* commented on a new ordinance passed in a midwestern city "forbidding taverns to sell liquor on the Sabbath to any persons except travellers. The next Sunday every man in town who wanted a nip was seen walking around with a valise in one hand and two carpetbags in the other."

A *nip* is a small drink, a taste of something, usually alcoholic. It comes from *nipperkin,* a drink of ale equivalent to about half a pint. By extension it came to mean anything small or brief.

Looking to clean up in more ways than one, casinos in Las Vegas know that many of their female customers "are the kind [sic] of girls who obey their mothers' warnings never to sit on strange toilet seats." Because of such fastidiousness, "attendants have to nip in after that type, making sure the next woman will have no unpleasant surprises" *(Time,* 27 August 1984, 6).

Noggin

My daugher Becky was in tears.

"What's the matter?" I asked, at the same time trying to soothe her.

"Jason." That's all she said. It was enough. Big brother (ten years old) had done something to her again.

This time he had given her a "noogy."

For aficionados of childhood tortures, to do a "noogy" you take your knuckles, press hard on the top of your victim's head, and rub back and forth.

It's called a "noogy" because the focus of pain is the head, otherwise called, since 1800, a "noggin," as in "that's using the old noggin."

Like *kopf,* the German word for "head," *noggin* originally was a cup or mug, a container for beer or ale. Its career started in the seventeenth century, but no one knows how it originated. The *Oxford English Dictionary* merely says, "of obscure origin."

The *nog* part of egg nog is obviously related. Today egg nog is a blend of eggs, milk, sugar, nutmeg, and an alcoholic beverage, usually rum. Originally nog was a beer brewed in East Anglia and characterized by a high alcohol content.

Pledge

The other day I turned on the public television channel and was greeted by a duo of fast-talking fundraisers cajoling me to pledge money so that the station could bring me the programs they said I wanted. If I didn't call, I might never again see programs like the previous one, they warned. But if I called and pledged $100, not only would I receive a paperback book that I could get for $3.50 at my local bookstore, but some anonymous donor would match my pledge dollar for dollar. The twosome begged and pleaded not to let this opportunity pass through my fingers.

Convinced that supporting this station and its embattled employees was my civic duty, I was about to reach for the phone and call the number shown at the bottom of the screen when the phone rang.

At the other end was another huckster asking me to pledge any amount I cared to for a charity that will remain nameless. While I was trying to refuse courteously, my wife yelled up from our laundry room that she had forgotten to tell me that the other day she had pledged $5 to help surviving veterans of the Spanish-American War or some other such group.

Pledging is like using credit cards. You don't realize you're spending money until the bill comes. Then you wonder how you accumulated such debt. However, money is not the only thing that can be pledged. Just a few centuries ago people used to pledge lives.

Our word *pledge* comes from Old French *plege,* "security," or "guarantee." It acquired its present meaning of promise as a consequence of the Danish invasion of England in the ninth century.

After the conquest, Englishmen were not allowed to drink in the presence of a Dane without expressed permission. To do so was considered wholly disrespectful and sometimes resulted in instant death. These killings so intimidated the English that they refused to drink in the company of Danes even when invited to, unless a Dane pledged his safety. This request for permission was an extension of the Danes' own custom of pledging, whereby the one about to drink asked whether the person seated next to him would "pledge" him. If agreed to, the latter would stand and hold up his knife or sword to protect the drinker against unexpected attack from a secret enemy. This was not a capricious request or custom, since many a Dane had his throat cut while drinking.

Later on, the custom of pledging to protect someone's life evolved into a pledge of friendship or love through drinking, as recorded in 1631 by Ben Jonson *(To Celia):* "Drink to me only with thine eyes, and I will pledge with mine." In the nineteenth century, pledging took on a whole new meaning in the wake of the rising temperance movement. Instead of a guarantee of safety, someone who "took the pledge" swore to abstain entirely from alcohol.

Porterhouse

Americans eat a lot of meat, especially steak when they can get it. One of the most popular cuts of steak is the "porterhouse." It's the section of beef located between the sirloin and the tenderloin.

Years before porterhouse referred to a cut of beef, it was a general name for a tavern or a beerhouse. This was due to the popularity of porter, a malt beer, during the 1700s and 1800s.

The brewer credited with first making porter in 1730 was an Englishman, Ralph Harwood. In Harwood's day, various mixtures of ale and beer had become popular, with "half and half" or "three threads" (a mixture of three different brews) especially in demand. To accommodate his customers, the brewer (who was also the bartender) had to take various portions from at least two different casks, a time-consuming and tiring process. To make it easier on himself, Harwood experimented with mixtures of the various ingredients, which he put into one cask or "butt." Harwood called this concoction "entire" or "entire butt." The name was appropriate, but it had no sales magic, so Harwood decided to rename it *porter.*

So far we are dealing with fact. Now comes the conjecture about why Harwood called it porter. One explanation is that porter was short for "porter's beer," and that Harwood simply named it after the many porters who liked his new concoction. Another story is that Harwood dispatched his employees with his ale to areas where porters worked, and these employees would announce their presence with a shout of "Porter!" meaning not the brew, but the customers for whom it was intended.

Porter soon became a favorite among the blue-collar workers of that era, and other brewers tried to gain their share of the market with similar innovations. The only one to last, however, was *stout,* a stronger version of porter which Dublin brewers seemed particularly adept at making.

Porter was unknown in the United States until the mass migrations from the United Kingdom. To meet the sudden and considerable demand, a new type of tavern opened which featured porter. These taverns were known as *porterhouses,* and along with the hearty porter, patrons were served steak and other meals. The cut of beef now known as "porterhouse" was named because it was the most common cut of beef sold at these porterhouses.

P's and q's

The other day I was in the supermarket with my 6-year-old daughter Becky, who single-handedly keeps Hershey and other candy makers in business. While we were walking near the checkout counter, one of the mothers in line yanked her own little one away from the candy display and in a stern tone admonished her to "mind your p's and q's."

Becky and I continued shopping, but while we were standing in line, she went over to the same candy display and meticulously examined every chocolate bar, package of gum, and roll of candy she could find. Finally she picked out Snickers, her favorite, and put it on the conveyor along with the other groceries we had harvested from the shelves.

"Looking for something else?" I asked as she took my hand and waited for the cashier to get to her chocolate bar.

"They didn't have any more," she answered, obviously disappointed.

"Any more what?"

"P's and Q's. That other girl got the last one. Are P's and Q's better than M and M's?"

"P's and q's aren't candy. Her mommy was just telling her to behave. She wasn't supposed to have any candy and she was disobeying."

Becky let out a soft "Oh," and then giggled at her mistake.

If, like the little girl, you were once told to "mind your p's and q's," you were told to be careful. You'd overstepped the rules set out for you, or you'd meddled where you weren't wanted.

Meddling in other people's affairs is as old as the snake in the Garden of Eden. "P's and q's" have a much shorter history, but one that still goes back several centuries to England's venerable pubs when ale was served by the pint or quart. A pub owner would keep track of how much he served his customer by "minding his p's (pints) and q's (quarts)" on a slate. In this way he kept a running tab. When the customer came to pay his bill, he paid according to the number of "p's and q's" the pub owner had "minded" for him.

Another explanation for "p's and q's" holds that it originated after John Shaw opened a famous punch house in Manchester, England, in 1739. Shaw served his punch in bowls of two sizes—a shilling bowl known as a *P* bowl, and a sixpenny bowl known as a *Q* bowl. Those who drank alone asked for *Q's;* parties of two or more asked for *P's.* Interesting though this story may be, it cannot be correct since *P* and *Q* (originally spelled Pee and Kew) go back to 1602 (although the expression "minding your p's and q's" dates to 1779).

Brewer's Dictionary of Phrase and Fable mentions yet another possible source, this one in France. During the reign of Louis XIV, it was *de rigeur* to wear a long wig, but this created a problem for the dancing set who sometimes stepped on their wigs while bending over to bow deeply. To avoid such a *faux pas,* the dance master warned his students to mind their p's (*pieds,* "feet") and q's (*queues,* "wigs").

And then there are those who contend that the expression began as an admonition to apprentice typesetters not to confuse the two letters, since the type face for each was the opposite of the printed letter.

Proof

Proof is a measure of alcohol content in distilled spirits. Legally, it is a mixture of alcohol in water resulting in a specific gravity of 12/13 at 51 degrees Fahrenheit. If the mixture has more alcohol, it is "overproof"; less alcohol, and it is "underproof."

Before sophisticated technology was invented to determine specific gravity or the quantity of alcohol in a drink, distillers would mix equal amounts of gunpowder and alcoholic beverage and attempt to ignite it. If the mixture didn't burn, there wasn't enough alcohol and it was underproof; if it burned brightly, it had too much alcohol and it was overproof. If it burned steadily and evenly, with a blue flame, it was "prooved," or "100 percent perfect." This meant that it was drinkable, not that it contained 100 percent alcohol. The actual alcohol content was about 50 percent, considered to be the greatest strength that anyone would voluntarily drink.

Another method of determining proof is by "reading the bead." To do this a moonshiner shakes a jar of distillate and watches the bubbles or "beads." Shaking causes the bubbles to make circles in the middle of the distillate before passing to the edge where they burst. If the bubbles distribute themselves half in the liquid and half out before bursting, the liquid is 100 proof. If more of the bubbles appear out of the liquid, the proof is higher. (*See also* Bead *and* Moonshine).

Punch

The era of mixed drinks in Western civilization did not begin until relatively recent times. Until the late Middle Ages, people generally took their ales, wines, or liquors "straight." But when Europeans started colonizing other parts of the world, they began to learn new customs. One of these was to mix alcoholic beverages with other substances to create new tasty drinks.

As a result of the colonization of India, Europeans discovered many different native foods and drinks, one of which was a popular drink known as "punch."

It was called *punch* for one of two reasons. The first holds that it was simply an Anglicized version of the Hindustani word *panch,* "five," and was so called because it contained five ingredients: lime juice, sugar, spices, water, and arrack, a local alcoholic drink. *(Punjab* has a common root and literally means "five rivers.") The second credits the name to the English practice of storing the concoction in "puncheons" (large casks). Gradually the practice of mixing five ingredients waned, and the word came to be applied to any mixed drink regardless of number or kind of ingredients.

The most famous *punch house* in England (as places serving punch were called to distinguish them from alehouses) was opened in the early 1700s in Manchester by a former soldier named John Shaw. Shaw had been stationed in India where he had learned to concoct a good-tasting punch. When he returned to England he opened a punch house which quickly became a favorite drinking and meeting place. So popular was it that Shaw did not even put up a sign, a very unusual circumstance in a country of signs. Another unusual characteristic of Shaw's punch house was its closing time—8:00 P.M.

Shaw was a creature of habit. He had kept soldiers' hours for so long in the army that he could not change when he became a civilian. At the sound of the chime, Shaw would enter one of the rooms of his punch house and in a loud and military tone announce: "Eight o'clock, gentlemen, eight o'clock." No entreaty for another drink, no matter how urgent, could budge him.

Usually his patrons grudgingly gathered their belongings and left at his signal. When this failed, Shaw relied on one of two tactics. He called to his sturdy female assistant Molly to bring his horsewhip, which he cracked loudly near the ear of any errant guest who dilly-dallied. Should this fail, Molly brought a pail of water and emptied it upon the floor. This ruined the patrons' shoes and got them moving before they became more inundated.

The expression *punch-drunk* has nothing to do with punch, nor does *pleased as punch* or the English periodical *Punch*. The latter two come from the name of the rascal Punch in "Punch and Judy." (*See also* Drunk *and* Neat.)

The real McCoy

Some years ago a minor scandal erupted when archaeologists found they had been hoaxed. In 1912, an amateur archaeologist brought some old bones to the British Museum. The bones were not just old; they seemed to be thousands of years old. They looked like human bones, but not exactly. A subsequent journey to the gravel pit at Piltdown, where the first bones were discovered, led to the discovery of more bones. Later that year the amateur archaeologist and the expert from the museum jointly announced the discovery of the "missing link," a creature part man, part ape.

For thirty years the discovery was hailed as one of the most important archaeological discoveries in the world. Then in 1949 another scientist conducted some experiments on the bone fragments. To his surprise, he found that they did not contain much fluorine although they had supposedly been buried for thousands of years in soil that was full of the mineral. Bones absorb fluorine from the earth, and the longer they are buried the more they absorb; thus, the absence of fluorine made some scientists smell a rat. Further examination showed that the bones had been stained to make them look old. It was true that they were part man and part ape but only because someone had taken human bones and mixed them with orangutan bones. The amateur archaeologist had fooled the experts, passing off a grab bag of altered bones as *the real McCoy.*

Even the *McCoy* of *the real McCoy* may not be genuine. One group of etymologists, among them slang expert Eric Partridge, says that Americans stole the name from the Scottish clan of *Mackay;* another contends it is as American as apple pie. Either way there is an alcoholic connection.

As proof of his theory, Partridge says that Robert Louis Stevenson, author of *Treasure Island, Doctor Jekyll and Mr. Hyde,* and many other popular books, in 1894 used *the real Mackay* in a letter as if it were so well known he did not have to explain its meaning. This, argues Partridge, gives the expression at least a nineteenth century date. Partridge then says that "the phrase has long—perhaps always—been associated with whiskey." Although he was not certain why there was such an association, Partridge tells us that north of Inverness (home of the Loch Ness monster) is Mackay country, also known as Scotland's whisky* country. When the firm of Mackay and Company went into business in 1903, they called one of their brands "real Mackay," possibly to take advantage of the fame of Mackay country whisky and to plug their own family name. Other companies in that part of Scotland also called their brands "real Mackay" although their family name was not Mackay. While the phrase did not originate in these brands, says Partridge, their popularity probably gave it added life. But in his own *Dictionary of Slang and Unconventional English,* Partridge dates the appearance of *the real Mackay* in 1929.

Stevenson may have used the phrase in the nineteenth century, but like most Britons, Americans did not begin to call anything *the real McCoy* or *Mackay* until the late 1920s; when they did, they always said *McCoy,* not *Mackay.*

In *A Hog on Ice and Other Curious Expressions,* Charles Funk attributes the eponym to a prize fighter of the 1890s named Kid McCoy. Funk claims that the phrase sprang out of a true incident. It seems McCoy was so good that lesser fighters called themselves "Kid McCoy," too. One night a barfly made some uncomplimentary remarks about McCoy, unaware that the real Kid McCoy was a few elbows down the bar. The bartender tried to warn him, but the loudmouth bragged he wasn't afraid of any fighter named McCoy and became more obnoxious. After the Kid decked him, he said he wasn't afraid of any McCoy except "the real McCoy."

There really was a Kid McCoy. He was born Norman Selby and won the welterweight championship in 1896. Later he put on more muscle and fought in the middleweight, light-heavyweight and heavyweight divisions, winning many fights but never the championship. By the second decade of the 1900s he was past his prime.

McCoy meant liquor as early as the first decade of the 1900s and probably did originate with the Kid, but it was always "the McCoy," never "the *real* McCoy."

---

* In Scotland, whiskey is always spelled "whisky."

This brings us to our next candidate, Bill McCoy.

During Prohibition many people made a lot of money either making "bathtub gin" (gin literally made in bathtubs of private homes) or smuggling it in from Canada where it was not illegal. From Canada, it was taken by boat to Rum Row, an offshore area outside U.S. territorial jurisdiction near New York, whence it was brought ashore. The operation was a dangerous one and demanded a fast boat that could hold a large cargo. The smugglers became known as rumrunners, and first among the lot was Captain Bill McCoy.

The bathtub gin and other varieties of Prohibition liquor made in the United States were vile concoctions, very often containing poisonous substances. They were not blended and of course there was no aging or quality control of any sort. The only requisite ingredient was alcohol. By contrast, liquor smuggled into the United States was quality brand material, much of it Canadian whiskey. There was simply no comparison.

McCoy not only founded Rum Row, he was its most successful rumrunner from 1921 to 1925. "His erstwhile associates," wrote his biographer F. Van de Water, "have epitomized his square crookedness in a phrase that has become part of the nation's slang: 'The real McCoy'—signifying all that is best and most genuine . . . a verbal monument to one who played a hazardous game daringly and, after his lights, fairly and honestly."

Prohibition was a turbulent era that stamped its mark on the nation in countless ways, language being only one of them. From its eponymous origins referring to high quality liquor, *the real McCoy* was applied to anything genuine or reputable.

There is one other possible claim to paternity, this one from the world of drugs. Americans have been using narcotics almost as long as alcohol, sometimes mixing the two in medicines, like laudanum. After the Civil War, there were so many veterans hooked on morphine that it seemed to many an epidemic had swept the nation. Narcotics were legal in the United States until they were outlawed in

1915. But this did not stop people from using them. In the 1940s, heroin was beginning to be imported on a large scale, but not all of it was of high quality. Heroin smuggled into the country from the island of Macao off the coast of China was an exception. It was usually undiluted and therefore highly prized by addicts who started referring to it as . . . you guessed it, "the real Macao."

"Sit [stand] like a Stoughton bottle."

In *Heavens to Betsy!* Charles Funk devotes several pages to this old New England expression, the only one, he claims, in which a distinctive bottle became a household word.

Sitting or standing like a Stoughton bottle means to act unconcerned or uninterested in what is going on or what is being said, like "a bump on a log."

Funk says that his father-in-law, a New England country doctor, used the expression often. My in-laws have lived in New England from the time it was first settled in 1620, but only my wife's grandmother, now in her nineties recalls ever hearing it. My father-in-law, who is in his sixties cannot remember having heard anyone say it, including his mother. Even if obsolete, this is an expression whose story is worth telling.

The Stoughton bottle contained a tonic or bitters made mainly with alcohol. It was named after an English apothecary named Stoughton, who was granted the second medicine patent to be issued in England. An advertisement for Dr. Stoughton's nostrum recommended using it "as often as you please," says Funk, "in a glass of 'Spring water, Beer, Ale, Mum, Canary (wine), White wine, with or without sugar, and a dram of brandy.'"

The expression was not based on the bottle's content or on the condition it induced in consumers if taken as recommended, but rather on the shape of the bottle. The appeal of the ingredients notwithstanding, the bottles were even more popular because they were large, made of stoneware, and had a flat side with flanges to keep them from rolling. When filled with hot water they served as convenient foot warmers during the cold New England winters. Apparently the English had other means of warming their feet, however, for the expression was never used in England, although Dr. Stoughton's elixir was very popular there.

Skid row

Every big city has its *skid row,* a rundown, dirty area populated by people who have no other place to go. Usually it is the part of town where drunken derelicts sleep and live. Although skid rows have been part of the American scene for a long time, they have only been so called since the mid-1800s.

The dubious honor of giving birth to the name goes to Seattle, Washington. In 1852, a saw mill was built in what was then known as Seattle's Pioneer Square district, near Puget Sound. To get timber to the saw mill, logs had to be pulled along tracks or skids located in what is now Yesler Way. Because of the skids, the area became popularly known as "skid road." As the logging business grew, other businesses, among them bars and cheap hotels, moved into the area to serve the loggers. Seattle continued to develop and prosper, but Pioneer Square failed to keep up, eventually becoming impoverished and relatively abandoned by commerce. Few concerned themselves about what went on there or who lived there, as long as skid row residents did not bother anyone in other parts of the city. "Road" was shortened to "row" and the area became known as "skid row," not inappropriately, considering the rows of vagrants and homeless drunks inhabiting the area.

Small beer

An insignificant person is *small beer*. It can also mean a trifling or something of little value. This characteristically British expression is derived not from a small quantity of beer, but from beer with a low alcohol content, hence its insignificance.

For commoner and royalty alike, beer and bread are the two most traditional items in the English diet. At the court of Henry VIII, breakfast consisted of "one chete loafe, one manchet, two gallons of ale, and a pitcher of wine." Chete loaf and manchet were types of bread. Beer and ale were also essential to any festivity and observance, religious or secular. It is because of all this drinking that the country was called "Merrie England" in medieval days:

> England was merry England when
> Old Christmas brought his sports again;
> 'Twas Christmas broached the mightiest ale,
> 'Twas Christmas told the merriest tale;
> A Christmas gambol oft would cheer
> A poor man's heart through half the year.
> (Sir Walter Scott, "Marmion")

Since beer was the staple of the English diet, it is hardly surprising that there were so many different qualities. Price depended on alcoholic content. Some of the strongest beers were called *dragon's milk, stingo* and *merry-go-down. Humming ale* was affectionately so called because it made the drinker's head hum. *Small beer* was the weakest variety, usually made by brewing malt a second time. Some people drank it the way we drink soda pop; hard drinkers called it *starve gut.*

By Shakespeare's time *small beer* was already a metaphor for anything inconsequential. When Iago describes a certain woman as a wight—a strong and valiant person—Desdemona asks "to do what?" To which Iago sarcastically replies, "to suckle fools and chronicle small beer" (*Othello,* 2.1.161). On the other hand, not to think oneself "small beer" is to have a good self-opinion, almost to the point of conceit. The expression, to my knowledge, never made it to America. Instead of *small beer,* Americans preferred *small potatoes,* probably because meat and potatoes are staples of the American diet.

Soda jerker

The only place one is likely to see a soda jerker these days is in an old movie. Until about the 1960s, drug stores used to have a counter or "fountain" where customers could sit and order a dish of ice cream, a soft drink, or a mixture of both called a soda. The person who served them was called a *soda jerker.* He was usually a clean-cut teenager garbed in a white uniform, who epitomzed sobriety and good-naturedness in everything but his name. There were no female soda jerkers.

The first soda jerkers dispensed beer, not soda. *Beer jerker* used to be slang for a drunkard who could not control his movements because of having drunk too much beer. In the latter part of the nineteenth century, people stopped calling drunks "beer jerkers" and instead started calling bartenders by that name. Later, when soda fountains proliferated, the counterpart of the "beer jerker" became "soda jerker."

Swig

When you take a *swig* of something, you gulp it down. A swig is a guzzle. It is not a sip. And it is usually of liquor.

Originally, swig was a popular seventeenth century drink made of spiced ale, wine, and toast. In 1732, a Sir Watkin Williams Wynn presented a silver ten-gallon bowl to Jesus College at Oxford. Used only on 1 March to commemorate St. David's Day, the bowl was filled with swig, and students were served from it using a ladle of half-pint capacity—not exactly a sip. Several years later, St. David's Day at Oxford was renamed "Swig Day" because of the custom.

The name of the drink and the large serving size gave rise to the present meaning of the word.

Symposium

Every scientific convention includes a special session called a *symposium* (plural *symposia*). Symposia are supposed to be opportunities to hear experts discuss the latest developments in their common speciality.

Symposia should never be attended by people who need to stay awake. They are soporifics. Insomniacs who want to be cured should consider attending these shindigs.

The ancient Greeks who invented the symposium would have been appalled at what we have done to their celebration of wit.

Symposium is a Latin word derived from Greek *syn,* "with" and *posis,* "drinking." In the days of the Ancient Greeks, a *symposion* was a lively and entertaining occasion. Everyone had fun and drank a lot of wine. When one of Plato's famous dialogues was translated into English in the sixteenth century, the translator thought "Symposium" an obvious title. What better name for a drinking party at which profound philosophical ideas—the nature of love, for example— were discussed? At another famous Symposium recorded by Plutarch, more mundane subjects were raised, such as how too much drinking affects sexual performance.

The Greek symposium had a formal structure. First, guests dined, usually without talking or drinking. When everyone had finished and the table had been cleared, wine was brought in. Cups were filled and everyone stood while the host poured out wine in honor of a god. The guests then uttered the symposion hymn in honor of Dionysus, god of wine. This hymn officially signalled the beginning of the symposium. Next, a toastmaster, known as the *symposiarch,* was chosen by a toss of the dice. Symposium etiquette required that participants all drink together and only when the symposiarch indicated. It was he who decided how much wine would be poured into a cup, how dilute it would be (the Greeks drank their wine straight only at breakfast), and how many cups of wine would be drunk. Because of these prerogatives, the symposiarch decided whether the symposium would turn into a drunken revel.

During the night the guests discussed lofty topics as well as mundane issues of the day, and every so often they took a break. Sometimes they sang songs or listened to music or played a game called *cattabos,* which involved pouring wine into a saucer a few feet away. As the contestant poured, he uttered his paramour's name; if the wine landed in the saucer, it was taken as a good sign for their affair.

The Romans carried on the tradition of the symposium in its basic form. They too began with an offering to the wine god, but they drank while they ate and eventually drank not to stimulate conversation but to get drunk. And whereas the Greeks had drunk in unison at large gatherings, the Romans drank whenever they wished and did so at private parties.

The often dry formality of the modern-day symposium bears only the faintest resemblance to the Greek *symposion.* Today, more commonly, it is during dinner following the symposium that the warm and convivial atmosphere of the Greek *symposion* still thrives, as colleagues now seated around a table (rather than in an auditorium-like setting) informally discuss lively issues.

Table beer

Table beer is an old and now forgotten British expression meaning "trifling, of no consequence." It is similar to *small beer.* Table beer originally was poor quality beer that was cheap and therefore affordable to those who could not otherwise purchase more expensive beer.

Take him down a peg.

This unusual expression has nothing to do with ladders. Instead it is a figurative expression meaning to humilitate someone or to deflate his ego. The idea is to cause someone to come down from the lofty position in which he has placed himself.

Peg is an old word for ale. It got the name because of a law introduced in the tenth century by the Saxon King Edgar at the urging of St. Dunstan. The Saxons drank out of large wooden communal tankards holding about two quarts. St. Dunstan thought that Saxons got drunk so often because they could not estimate how much they were taking from the tankards. To help make sure judgments, Dunstan ordered eight wooden pegs or pins to be inserted at equal intervals in all tankards. This divided the contents into eight half-pint draughts. Each drinker was supposed to drink up to a peg and then pass the tankard:

> Come, old fellow, drink down to your peg!
> But do not drink any farther, I beg.
> (Longfellow, "Golden Legend," iv)

Instead of restraining drinking, the peg tankard encouraged drinkers to see who could drink more pegs. Taking someone down a peg originally meant going one's competitor one better by drinking one more peg or half-pint than he. By extension, the expression took on the meaning of humbling someone.

Two related expressions are: *I'm a peg too low,* and *to peg away at it.* The first means "I'm feeling depressed." Originally it meant "I feel sad and need a drink (a peg of ale) to make me feel better." Having had that drink and a few more besides, a drinker's mood might change, and instead of being sad, he might find himself *in merry pin,* i.e., cheerful as a result of drinking several "pins" of ale.

To peg away at something means to persist no matter how many discouraging setbacks are encountered. It too comes from the peg tankard at which the drinker "pegged away" until he consumed its entire contents.

Tap

Miners or prospectors sometimes talk about *tapping* a vein, by which they mean extracting gold or silver from a ridge of the precious mineral found in the earth. By analogy, if you've spent all your money, you may say that you are *tapped out.* While we don't use *tapped* when talking about giving blood, a nose bleed resulting from a fight is sometimes called a *tap.* A punch on the nose is called a *tap* for the same reason—blood is drawn. In the nineteenth century this was called *tapping the claret.*

Years ago tavern owners were called *tapsters,* since they were always *tapping* or drawing ale from a cask. By the same token those who drank a lot were also known as tapsters. People whose last name is *Tapster, Tapester,* or *Tapper* are related, not to the over-indulging customers, but to former tavern owners whose lot it was to open casks.

Tapping the admiral. *See* Nelson's blood

Taps, tattoo

Unless you've been in the army, a *tattoo* is something engraved into your skin. For a soldier, a *tattoo* is a drum or bugle call summoning him back to camp. Another bugle call known as *taps* tells him it is time to turn off barrack lights and go to bed. In 1824, Congress even mandated an orderly's duty: "to visit his rooms at taps; see that the lights are extinguished; the fires properly secured; the occupants present, and in bed."

Every army has needed some formal signal for getting its troops back to camp and to bed, but why are these signals known as *tattoo* and *taps*? The answer is that before the word was *tattoo*, it was variously spelled and pronounced as *tap-too, tap too,* and *taptow,* the latter being taken directly from the Dutch word *taptoe.* The Dutch word is comprised of two elements, *tap,* "the tap-hole or opening of a cask,' and *toe,* meaning "shut." *Tattoo* literally means "shut the tap-hole on the cask."

The *Oxford English Dictionary* gives the year 1644 as the earliest recorded instance of the word in English. It was found in a directive issued by a Colonel Hutchinson: "If anyone shall bee found tiplinge or drinkinge in any Taverne, Inne, or Alehouse after the houre of nyne of the clock at night, when the Tap-too beates, hee shall pay 2s,6d."

Taps, the summons to go to bed, is merely a variant of *tattoo.*

Teetotaler

For almost as long as alcohol has been around it has had its opponents. When the first groups were organized in the early 1800s to reduce the amount of drinking, they were called "temperance" societies or unions. Most members of these groups were not initially against all drinking; they just wanted to cut down on the amount of "hard drinking," that is the drinking of whiskey and rum. But hard liners eventually took over and began to demand total abstinence.

During one of the meetings of a British temperance group in 1833, total abstinence was again raised as an issue. According to one account, a hardliner named Dick Turner, argued that complete abstinence was the only way sobriety could be guaranteed. Because Turner stuttered when nervous, instead of saying what he had intended, he said "n-n-nothing but tee-tee-total abstinence will do." Opponents of total abstinence immediately began to refer to the position as "teetotalism" in mockery, but instead of backing off, supporters also adopted it because it sounded more emphatic.

Apparently the disagreement went so deep that Turner's supporters felt they had to do something special to acknowledge coinage of the word; thus when Turner died they had his tombstone inscribed with this epitaph:

> Beneath this stone are deposited the remains of Richard Turner, author of the word *Teetotal* as applied to abstinence from all intoxicating liquors, who departed this life on the 27th day of October, 1846, aged 56 years.

But there is another story about *teetotal* that places its origins in Hector, New York, several years before the English episode (1827).

According to this version, the New York Temperance Society also debated the issue of abstinence. The original pledge to which members swore when they joined the Society stipulated: "No member shall drink rum, gin, whiskey, wine, or any distilled spirits, or compositions of the same, or any of them, except by the advice of a physician, or in case of actual disease . . . under penalty of twenty-five cents."

Some of the members wanted to eliminate the loophole that exempted beer. The Society was split on the issue. To indicate which side a member endorsed, each wore badges bearing the initials *O.P.,* meaning Old Pledge, i.e., abstention from distilled spirits only, or *T* meaning total abstinence. The latter was eventually referred to as *T-total.* By 1832 Americans were already using the word apart from its connection with alcohol to mean "utterly or completely": "These Mingoes . . . ought to be essentially, and particularly, and tee-totally obflisticated off of the face of the whole earth" (*New English Dictionary*). By 1844 *teetotally* had become so hackneyed that journalists jeered at those who used it: "'Tee-totalism' is a term no longer mentioned, excepting in the journals of distant towns and foreign lands, or perhaps in some jesting lyric listened to with laughter from the stage" (Philadelphia *Spirit of the Times,* 10 September 1844).

But it was too playful a word to die quickly, and Americans kept it alive until the turn of the century.

Three sheets to the wind

In the days of the great windjammers the amount of sail on a ship determined how fast it could go. But to be effective the sail had to be securely fastened so it could catch the wind. To do this, the sailor pulled down on the ropes, called "sheets," attached to the corners of the sail and tied them tightly. An untied sail would flap uncontrollably in the wind, and the ship would be disabled. By analogy, sailors referred to the staggering, uncontrollable gait of a drunken sailor in terms of a number of sheets in the wind.

One sheet to the wind meant a sailor was slightly drunk, but still able to perform his duties; if *two sheets to the wind,* he was quite drunk and could barely hold his own; *three sheets to the wind* meant that he was totally drunk, unable to walk at all without staggering; and *four sheets to the wind* meant he was unconscious.

According to lexicographer Eric Partridge, the more common of the four expressions, surfaced in the 1820s. It was colloquial for about a century, and then finally became standard English. Because most people who use it are not seamen, they often make the mistake of thinking that a *sheet* is a sail rather than a rope.

Tip

According to folk-etymology, the origin of tipping and the word *tip* goes back to the early days of the tavern.

In colonial days, the tavern was often the center of a town's activities. It was hospitable and homey, a place to meet, talk, and relax as well as to stay overnight when journeying between towns. There were bedrooms, a living room, and of course a taproom. The taproom often had a roaring fire where patrons could warm themselves on a cold night, a desk where letters could be written, tables for playing cards or checkers, and barrels and bottles.

When taverns were small, they were family-run and -operated businesses. When they got bigger, waiters had to be hired. These early waiters brought food and drink to customers just as they do today. In return they received a small salary from the tavern owner. To increase their earnings, they solicited something extra from those they waited on, not brazenly, mind you, but possibly through a subtle hint about the T.I.P. box (abbreviation for "to insure promptness"), the monies from which they shared. The box became known as the tip box, and although it eventually disappeared, the custom of tipping the waiter remained.

Entertaining though this folk etymology may be, tipping and the word *tip* predate colonial tavern days by quite a bit. Farmer and Henley (*Slang and Its Analogues*) cite the first recorded appearance of *tip* as gratuity in 1610, several years before the Pilgrims landed.

Tippler

Tipple means to drink to excess. A *tippler* is a boozer, someone who drinks a lot. *Tipple* and *tippler* are words not encountered very much any more. They have been replaced by a thousand other words with the same meaning. But *tipple* and *tippler* have left their mark in the telephone book.

Originally, this family name sprang from the occupation of *tippler,* a medieval tavern owner or beer seller (from the Middle English word, *tipeler*). During the Middle Ages people had to be licensed to work at particular jobs, even one that involved nothing more than selling beer. Brewer, in his *Dictionary of Phrase and Fable,* cites an ordinance dated 1577 which specifies that five men were appointed "tipplers of Lincoln beer," and no "other tippler [might] draw or sell beer" under penalities.

Because the *tippler* has always worked with beer, the word came to be associated with drinking the stuff as well as serving it.

Toast, toast of the town

In its review of the movie, *The Muppets Take Manhattan, Newsweek* magazine (30 July 1984) said, "This time Kermit [the frog] leads his troupes to Broadway, where they hope to become the toast of the town with a new musical."

Toast brings to mind a heated piece of bread on which butter and jelly are sometimes spread. It tastes good, but it's hardly anything to get excited about. Even French toast, a great favorite of millions at breakfast time, made by dipping bread in egg and heating it in a pan, is not the stuff dreams are made of.

The conventional use of *toast* entered English about the fourteenth century from Old French *toster,* derived from Latin *tostum,* past participle of the verb *torrere,* "to parch." Now, no one burns or parches anyone or anything when they offer a toast, so how did the word come to mean a salutation? The answer has more to do with custom than with etymology.

During the Middle Ages, most people drank beer and ale. Those who could afford to also liked a little wine now and then. But in those days wine did not taste very good, and it usually went bad very rapidly. To make it more palatable, wine drinkers would soak pieces of spiced toast in it as in Shakespeare's "Go fetch me a quart of sack, put a toast in't" (*Merry Wives,* 3.5). After drinking the wine, they ate the toast.

Today, sentiments about the good health of the host are offered when wine is consumed at parties, a custom called *toasting.* This practice may have originated in a roundabout way from the practice of soaking toast with wine. In 1709 an English magazine, the *Tatler,* contained an anecdote tracing the custom to an event during the reign of Charles II of England. A good-looking girl, says the *Tatler,* was standing in a pool of water during a public celebration. One of the men in the crowd filled a cup with some of the pool water and drank to her health. A slightly tipsy onlooker had a different idea; he jumped into the bath vowing that while he didn't care much for the liquor, he was going to have the toast. There was no toast for him that day, but *toasting* a lady in the sense of paying homage to her while drinking became popular around that time.

The custom soon was institutionalized in England, taking the form of our modern-day beauty contest. Says the *Tatler:*

> Though this institution had so trivial a beginning, it is now elevated into a formal order; and that happy virgin who is received and drank to at their meetings, has no more to do in this life, but to judge and accept of the first good offer. The manner of her inauguration is much like that of the choice of a Doge in Venice: it is performed by balloting; and when she is so chosen, she reigns indisputably for that ensuing year; but must be reelected anew to prolong her empire a moment beyond it. When she is regularly chosen, her name is written with a diamond on a drinking-glass. The hieroglyphic of the diamond is to show her, that her value is imaginary; and that of the glass to acquaint her, that her condition is frail, and depends on the hand which holds her.

Having explained the custom, the *Tatler* then describes the two reigning toasts of 1709:

> The foremost of the whole rank of toasts, and the most undisputed in their present empire, are Mrs. Gatty and Mrs. Frontlet: the first, an agreeable; the second, an awful beauty. These ladies are perfect friends, out of a knowledge that their perfections are too different to stand in competition. He that likes Gatty can have no relish for so solemn a creature as Frontlet; and an admirer of Frontlet will call Gatty a maypole-girl. Gatty forever smiles upon you; and Frontlet disdains to see you smile. Gatty's love is a shining quick flame; Frontlet's a slow wasting fire. Gatty likes the man that diverts her; Frontlet him who adores her. Gatty always improves the soil in which she travels; Frontlet lays waste the country. Gatty does not only smile, but laughs at her lover; Frontlet not only looks serious,

but frowns at him. All the men of wit . . . are professed servants of Gatty; the politicians and pretenders give solemn worship to Frontlet. Their reign will be best judged of by its duration. Frontlet will never be chosen more; and Gatty is a toast for life.

Toasting women by drinking to their health and toasting in general did not begin in the Middle Ages but dates back to Greek and Roman times when it was common practice to drink to the health of the gods. The Vikings also wished their gods well when they drank. Scandinavian hospitality dictated that people going from town to town be invited into homes on the way to warm themselves out of the frigid weather and to eat and drink. Usually the refreshment was a bowl of warm beer, a fixture in the Scandinavian home. The bowl was called a *skoal*. After the guest had seated himself by the fire and had thawed out a bit, his host would point to the bowl and ask "Skoal?" meaning "Would you like a drink from the skoal?" From this word for bowl came the general Scandinavian expression for a toast.

Toasting was in fact the rule rather than the exception at parties. Writing in his diary on 19 June 1663, Samuel Pepys reports that he went "to the Rhenish wine house, where Mr. Moore showed us the French manner when a health is drunk, to bow to him that drunk to you, and then apply yourself to him, whose lady's health is drunk, and then to the person you drink to, which I never knew before; but it seems it is now the fashion." Another Englishman, Lord Cockburn wrote in 1856 that "every glass during dinner had to be dedicated to someone. It was thought sottish and rude to take wine without this, as if forsooth there was no one present worth drinking with."

The practice of dipping toast in wine or beer eventually disappeared, perhaps because the wine got better or because people preferred to drink the wine rather than put it on bread. Toasting, in the sense of drinking to someone's health or to some sentiment or event, however, is still very much a part of any celebration. *Time* magazine remarked that among President Reagan's many talents, "No one is better at toasting the good times than Ronald Reagan, and few other

Presidents have invested quite so much political capital in doing so" (18 February 1985, 19).

There are literally thousands of toasts. The Scandinavians have their *skoal,* approximating "I salute you"; In Spanish-speaking countries the toast is *salud.* The French have *a votre sante;* the Italians, *alla tua salute;* and the Germans and Austrians, *prosit,* all of which mean "to your health." Jews toast each other with *l'chiam,* "to life;" the Russians say *za vashe z-dorovye,* "to your health;" and the Chinese, *kan pe,* "bottoms up." The most popular toasting expression in England is *cheers.* The United States has no official toast so people keep inventing new ones, as Humphrey Bogart did in the 1942 movie *Casablanca,* when he lifted his glass to Ingrid Bergman and said, "Here's looking at you, kid." (*See also* Symposium.)

Toastmaster

Closely related to *toasting* is the office of *toastmaster.* The toastmaster was originally known as the "tablemaster." His job was to insure that everyone at a party got a chance to talk. Since drinking has a tendency to loosen tongues, making some people more talkative than usual, the position of tablemaster was socially important. And since drinking also makes certain people belligerent, it was a job requiring tact.

One of the activities at parties, as has already been mentioned in connection with banqueting, was the wishing of good will and health to particular ladies. Each man often had at least one lady in mind, and so a good tablemaster had to see that everyone had the opportunity to wish his lady's health. After the ladies came to be known as *toasts,* the office of tablemaster became toastmaster in accord with this special emphasis of his role.

Tumbler

A *tumbler* is a glass, usually a large one. Although it now has no particular association with alcohol, the word goes back to the sixteenth century before flat-bottomed glasses were invented.

In those days drinking vessels were often made out of horn with lead affixed to the bottom. It was an early Anglo-Saxon custom to consume the entire contents of a horn in one draught. To keep drinkers honest, drinking horns had rounded bottoms so they could not be set down without falling over and spilling their contents. When glasses were introduced, they too were often made with a round bottom; they could stand only when turned upside down. Otherwise they would *tumble* over. Later generations were not as adept at drinking and preferred to drink in smaller draughts; thus lead weights were added to the bottoms of glasses to keep them upright.

Two bits

When I was a boy, my friends and I used to sing a song that went:

> Shave and a haircut
> Two bits.
> Who was the barber?
> Tom Mix.
> What did he shave with?
> Toothpicks.
> Shave and a haircut
> Two bits.

I remembered this piece of nostalgia while watching an old western movie on television with my 10-year-old son Jason. Out of curiosity I asked him if he knew who Tom Mix was.

He didn't. What's more, he didn't know who Hopalong Cassidy

was, or Don Red Barry, or Wild Bill Elliot, or any of my favorite cowboy heroes.

"How about two bits?" I asked. "You know what two bits are?"

"Sure," he said, "it's two binary digits like 0 or 1. It's how the computer works."

At this point I knew I was entering foreign territory and figured I had better not go any further. "Yeah, right," I answered, and we both went back to watching the movie.

While many people of my age (forty-three) may still remember "shave and a haircut" and know that "two bits" meant twenty-five cents, very few, including me, are old enough to have ever seen a *bit* token. These tokens were a form of currency found in English and Mexican taverns which came to be used in American saloons in frontier days. During the 1870s when America was experiencing a prosperity boom, beer jumped from ten cents a glass to two glasses for twenty-five cents. Customers usually ordered two beers at a time, but because the glasses were very large, customers often couldn't drink more than one. Since bartenders couldn't give twelve and a half cents in change, they started giving out a form of the modern day "due bill" called "bar chits," "beer chips," or *bit* tokens. *Two bits* was token money for twenty-five cents. On one side of it was printed the name of the saloon along with an inscription such as "good for one drink," or "good for one shot of red eye."

Vinegarish, vinegar

When I was a boy we had a neighbor who did not get along very well with the other people on our street. My parents were friendly with everyone else, yet they hardly ever talked to this man except for an occasional "hello." My father said that this neighbor hadn't always been so "vinegarish," but something had happened to him that changed him almost overnight.

I never found out what had caused the change. But at the time I thought my father's description of our neighbor as "vinegarish" was a little strange, since having grown up in Canada where people still enjoy the English habit of sprinking vinegar instead of ketchup on their "chips" (french fries), I thought of vinegar as something I liked. Many years later I came across the word again and looked it up. What my father had meant in calling our neighbor vinegarish was that he was caustic and sour, just like vinegar.

Vinegar is derived from two French words, *vin* (wine) and *aigre* (sour or bitter). Like my neighbor, it starts off pleasant enough, but turns unpleasant if not kept properly.

Wassail

An odd word heard mainly at Christmas time is *wassail,* as in the old Christmas carol, "Here We Come A-wassailing." Perhaps if the carolers knew what they were singing, they might drop this one from their repertoire.

Wassail comes from the Anglo-Saxon greeting, *was hal,* which in turn comes from Old Norse and meant "be hale," or healthy. When Norsemen drank they toasted one another with "Hail!" meaning good health. The English word "health" in fact is derived from the Norse word. When the Anglo-Saxon inhabitants took over the vocabulary of the Norsemen who had invaded England, one of the words they adopted was *hail* changing it to *hael* and adding the word, *waes,* meaning "be".

English legend traces the expression to an event in 450 A.D. During a party given by the Saxon King Hengist for the British King Vortigern, Hengist's beautiful daughter Rowena filled a goblet with wine, knelt, and wished the king good health—"Liever Kyning, Wass-hael!" King Vortigern did not understand what she meant and had his servant explain the toast. The king liked what he heard almost as much as what he saw, and he kissed Rowena and had her sit by his side. From then on "wass hael" became a drinking pledge meaning "be healthy." "Wass hael" eventually became *wassail.*

The *wassail bowl* was a large bowl containing spiced ale. During the early Middle Ages, young girls visited friends and relatives on Christmas eve carrying a wassail bowl with them. Those visited were invited to drink the ale. In return, they gave a donation to the church for the coming year. "Here we come a-wassailing," refers to the practice of bringing the wassail bowl to someone's home.

People who drink too much are still called *wassailers* in memory of the large bowls of ale consumed during the holidays. (*See also* Loving cup.)

Wet your whistle

Derived from *whet,* meaning to moisten, and *whistle,* a colorful word for throat, this is a very old expression meaning "have a drink," usually but not necessarily one containing alcohol. The expression dates to 1386 and Chaucer's *Canterbury Tales:* "As any jay she light was and jolyf, / So was hir joly whistle wel ywet" ("The Reeve's Tale," 4154, 4155). It also appears in Pastores' *Townley Mysteries* written in 1400: "Had she oones wett hyr whystyll she couth syng fulle clere."

Wet your whistle is probably our oldest recorded expression for taking a drink. Here are several dozen more, many of which have seen better days:

absorb	gargle	go feed the goldfish
belly up	gas up	go see a dog about
bend your elbow	gasp	a man
bezzle	gin up	go see a marine
bib	give a bottle a	go see Baby
bibble	black eye	grog up
breathe a prayer	give a Chinaman a	guttle
fire a slug	music lesson	hang one on

have a drink
have your spot hit
have a swill
h'ist one
hob or nob
inhale alki
irrigate
jug up
lap it up
let us drive
  another nail
let us get there
liquor
moisture
name it
name yours
name your poison
nominate your pizen
prime yourself
put on the bag
put on the barrel
put your name
  in the pot
see a clove
shake a cloth
shave the guts

shed a tear
shellac your tonsils
shoot
shout
siphon
slop down
slough up
sluice your bold
smash a brandy peg
sniff the cork
snort
soak your chaffer
splice the main brace
sponge up
stimulate
suck your face
sugar the kidney
take a drop
take a jolt
take a nip
take an oath
take a pull
take a shot
take a shot in
  the arm

take a shove in
  the guts
take a shove in
  the mouth
take a slug
take a smell
take a sneak
take a snifter
take a snort
take a wet
take some cheer
take something for
  the stomach
take your medicine
tank up
tap the admiral
tip
toss
tune up
up the bucket
wattle
wet the clay
wet the other eye
wet the sickle
wipe off your chin

Whiskeybroom 'with'

This peculiar expression is a product of the pre-Prohibition era. It appeared around 1897. Originally it meant "drunkenness;" eventually it came to mean any kind of subterfuge.

The story behind the expression has as its protagonist Miss

Kate Field, an ardent prohibitionist in the late nineteenth century. Miss Field was on a speaking tour in Kansas, a dry state, and went into the drug store for a whisk broom that was displayed in the window.

"With or without?" asked the owner.

"What do you mean?" Miss Field asked, a little bewildered at such an unusual question.

The owner held up two apparently identical whisk brooms. Then, with a mischievous twinkle, he parted the wisps of one of the brooms, revealing a flask. A little twirl of his thumb and finger and the top of the "broom" came off.

Miss Field bought both brooms, one for its intended purpose, the other to illustrate her lecture "Does Prohibition Prohibit?" first given on 8 July 1897.

The annals of liquor lore are full of subterfuges. Perhaps the best known of these are the *blind pig,* the *striped pig,* and various offshoots like the *blind tiger.* These illegal liquor outlets appeared in the aftermath of the growing temperance movement in the United States during the 1830s. Frustrated in their efforts to make the country give up booze voluntarily, the temperance crusaders embarked upon prohibition. First they imposed their views through local option licensing. Next they persuaded various state legislatures. Finally in 1919 they succeeded in having booze outlawed throughout the land.

But along the way various loopholes in the laws were discovered. Like the one in the Massachusetts statutes of 1838 prohibiting the sale of booze but saying nothing about giving it away free. So one entrepreneur "gave it away." But to get it the recipient had to pay an admission price of six cents to see a striped pig. The pig was just an ordinary pig on whose sides our hero had painted some stripes. The ploy circumvented the law and spawned various other subterfuges until these too were outlawed.

White lightning

This is a clear white alcohol distillate produced by a moonshiner. Two possible origins for the term have been suggested. The first is based on the color and potency of the drink; the second derives from an early nineteenth century belief in two kinds of lightning: white and red, or bluish-red. Fires started by white lightning were believed to be unextinguishable because they were too hot, while those started by the other could be extinguished because they were cooler.

The inferno in the stomach that followed drinking this particular raw, unaged, clear alcohol distillate was named after the hotter, unquenchable lightning.

The whole shebang

Referring to rock singer David Lee Roth's purchase of an opulent estate in Pasadena, *People* magazine (11 February 1985, 118) said that "the whole shebang" was "surrounded by imposing walls, wrought iron gates and a sign bearing the greeting, 'There is nothing here worth dying for. No trespassing.'"

A *shebang* isn't exactly a wealthy estate. It's a lot lower on the architectural totem pole of opulence.

The source of this unusual expresssion is Ireland, and true to the stories about the Irish, it comes with a drink. In Ireland, a tavern or public house that catered to the lower class or to a disreputable clientele was called a "shebeen," from Gaelic *seibin,* meaning a quantity of liquor, like a dram or quart, or a container. The *Irish House of Commons Journal* for 1762 reports that the Limerick District Committee was informed by a local citizen that "he saw a Sheebeen which held two Ale Quarts made Use of in the Markets."

Shebeen came to America with the Irish, and by the 1860s it was Americanized to *shebang. The whole shebang* first meant downing the entire contents of a drinking vessel, but then it referred to the entire contents of anything—a pitcher, a house, someone's personal wealth, or even a book. Just as you, dear Reader, have now finished *the whole shebang*.

Appendix

This is my list of synonyms for the word *drunk*.

about done
about full
about gone
about had it
about right
about shot
a-buzz
account, casting
  up his
aced
activated
addled
adrip
afflicted
afloat
aglow
alcoholized
alecie
ale-washed
alight
alkied
alkied up

alky soaked
all at sea
all geezed up
all gone
all in
all liquored-up
all lit-up
all mops and brooms
all out
all sails spread
all schnozzled
all there
all wet
almost frozen
altogethery
anchored in sot's bay
angel-altogether
antifreezed
antiseptic
aped
ape drunk
asotus

ass on backwards
at ease
at rest
awash
awry-eyed
Bacchus-bulged
Bacchus-butted
back home
bagged
baked
balmy
bamboozled
bang through
  the elephant
baptized
bar, over the
barleysick
barmy
barreled (up)
barrel fever
barrelhouse drunk
bashed

basted
batted
battered
batty
bay, over the
bears, see the
been among the
  Phillipians
been among the
  Philistines
been at an
  Indian feast
been at Barbados
been at Geneva
been in a storm
been in the
  bibbing plot
been in the
  crown office
been in the sauce
been in the sun
been to a funeral
been to France
been to Jericho
been to Olympus
been to the saltwater
been to free
  with Sir John
been too free with
  the creature
  strawberry
been with
  Sir John Goa
beerified

beer soaked
befuddled
beginning to fly
behind the cork
belly up
belted
bending over
bent
bent an elbow
bent and broken
bent out of shape
besot
bewildered
bewottled
beyond salvage
bezzled
bibacious
bibulous
biled owl
biffy
biggy
bingoe
bit
bit by a fox
bit his grannan
bit his name in
bit on
bit teed
bit tiddley
bit tipsy
bit wobbly
bite in the brute
bitten by a
  barn mouse

blanked
blasted
blighted
blimped
blind
blind drunk
blinded
blink, on the
blinking drunk
blinky
blissed
blistered
blithered
blitzed
bloated
block and block
blowed
blown
blown away
blown over
blown up
blowzy blue
blue around the gills
blue eyed
blued
boggled
bowzered
boxed
brained
brass eye, have a
breaky leg
breezy
brewer's basket, stole
  a manchet out of a

brick in his hat,
  got a
bridgey
bright eyed
brook, pissed in the
bruised
bubbed
bubbled
buckled
budgey
buffy
bug-eyed
bulge
bummed
bumpsie
bumpsy
bun
bun on, have a
bung-eyed
bunged
bungy
bunned
buoyant
burdocked
buried
burn with a low
  (blue) flame
burried
burst
business on both
  sides of the way
busky
busted
buzzed

buzzey
buzzy
cached
caged
came home by the
  villages
canned (up)
canon
can't hit the ground
  with his hat
can't see through
  a ladder
can't sport a
  right light
can't walk a chalk
cap sick
capable
capers, cuts his
cargoed
carrying a heavy load
carrying a load
carrying two
  red lights
cast
cat
catched
catsood
caught
cellar, he's in the
chagrined
chapfallen
charged
cheary
cherubimical

chickery
chipper
chirping merry
chocked
chucked
clear out
clinched
coagulated
coarse
cocked
cocked as a log
cocked to the gills
cockeyed
coguy
colored
comboozelated
comboozled
commin' (on)
completely gone
completely out of it
completely squashed
concerned
Concord, half way to
conflummoxed
corned
cornered
coxy-foxy
cracked
crackling
cramped
crapulous
crashed
crazed
crazy

creamed
crocked
crocko
crocus
cronk
crooked
cropsick
crosseyed
crowning office,
  in the
crump
crump fooled
crumped (out)
crying jag
cuckooed
cup too much
cupped
cups, in his
cupshot
curved
cushed
cut
cut in the craw
D and D
daffy
dagged
damaged
damp
dark day with him
dead to the world
decayed
deck(s) awash
deep cut
deep drunk

defaced
demoralized
derailed
detained on business
devil, seen the
dew drunk
dewed
diddled
ding swizzled
dinged
dingy
dinky
dipped
dipsy
dirtfaced
discombobulated
discomboobulated
discouraged
discumfuddled
disguised
dished
dish, got a
disorderly
distinguished
dithered
dizzy
do a Daniel Boone
do an edge
dog, killed his
done a Falstaff
done an Archie
done over
done up
doped

doped over
dotted
dotty
double-headed
double-tongued
doubled-up
down and out
down for the count
down with the fish
drunk in his dumpes
drunkok
drunkulent
drunky
due for drydock
dull-eyed
dumped
ears are ringing
ebrios
ebrious
edge
edged
edge on, have an
electrified
elephant's trunk
elevated
eliminated
embalmed
entered
exalt
exalted
example, made an
exhilarated
extinguished
faced

feel aces
feel dizzy
feel frisky
feel glorious
feel good
feel happy
feel his booze
feel his liquor
feel juiced-up
feel the effect
feeling no pain
fettered
feverish
fiddle-cup
fiddled
fired-up
fishey
fish-eyed
fishy
fishy about the gills
fishy-eyed
fixed
fizzed
fizzled
flag is out
flaked out
flakers
flako
flared
flat out drunk
flatch-kennurd
flawed
floating
flood one's sewers

flooded
flooey
floopy
floored
florid
florious
flostered
fluffy
flummixed
flush
flushed
fluster
flusterate
flusterated
flustered
flusticate
flusticated
fly-blown
fly high
flying blind
flying high
flying light
flying on one wing
flying the ensign
fogged
foggy
fogmatic
folded
foolish
forward
fossilized
four sheets in
  (to) the wind
fox, caught a

fox-drunk
foxy
fractured
frazzled
free and easy
fried
fried on both sides
friend, spoke with his
froze his mouth
frozen
fucked over
fuddle one's cap
fuddle one's nose
fuddled
fuddled as an ape
full
full as a boot
full as a bull
full as a fiddler
full as a goat
full as a goose
full as a lord
full as a tick
full as an egg
full of hops
full cargo
full-cocked
full-flavored
full of courage
full to the bung
full up
funny feeling
fully soused
fully tanked

fur-brained
fur on his tongue
fuzzled
fuzzy
fuzzy-headed
gaffed
gaga
gage
gaged, boozed the
galvanized
gargled
gaseous
gassed
gassy
gay
gayed
geared-up
geed
geeded
geed-up
geesed
generous
Geneva, been at
George, been before
get a bun on
get a glow on
get a jag on
get a load on
get a shithouse on
get a skate on
get a snootful
get a thrill
get an edge on
get barreled up

get bleary-eyed
get blotto
get boozed-up
get bung-eyed
get boozy
get canon
get charged-up
get crocked
get cut
get dopy
get flushed
get full
get glorious
get goofy
get high
get jungled
get light-headed
get likkered-up
get lit
get loaded
get looped
get loose
get organized
get pickled
get right
get shot
get sloppy
get soused
get stiff
get tanked-up
get the big head
get the gage up
get there with
   both feet

get topsy
get warmed
get wasted
get wet
get whizzy
get woozy
giddy
gizzled
gild
gilded
gill, blue around the
gills, filled to the
gills, green
   around the
gills, loaded to the
gin-crazed
gingered
ginned
ginny
glad
glaized
glanders
glassy, got the
glassy-eyed
glazed
globular
glorious
glowed
glowing
glow on
glued
god-awful drunk
good and drunk
gowed to the gills

had a couple
  of drinks
had a dram
had a few too many
had a little
had a little too many
had a snort
had his cold tea
had one or two
hair on his tongue
haily gaily
half-canned
half-cocked
half-corked
half-corned
half-crocked
half-cut
half-geared
half-gone
half-goofed
half in the bag
half in the boot
half-jacked
half-lit
half-loaded
half-looped
half-mocus
half-muled
half-on
half-out
half-pickled
half-pissed
half-rats
half-rinsed

half-screwed
half-seas over
half-shaved
half-shot
half-slewed
half-snaped
half-sober
half-soused
half-sprung
half-stewed
half-stiff
half-tanked
half the bay over
half the bay under
half-tipsy
half-under
half up the pole
halfway to Concord
hammered
hammerish
hanced
happy
has a bag on
has a brass eye
has a brick
  in one's hat
has a bun on
has a can on
has a drop in his eye
has a full cargo
has a glow on
has a guest
  in the attic
has a jag on

has a load on
has a package on
has a shine on
has a skate on
has a slant on
has a snoot full
has an edge on
has business on
has the screaming
  meemies
has the whoops
  and jingles
has the zings
hat, got on his little
haunted with evil
  spirits
hazy
head, got by the
hearing the owl hoot
heeled
heels a little
het-up
hiccius-doccius
hiccus
hickey
hiddey
high
high as a fiddler
high as a
  Georgia pine
high as a kite
high as Lindbergh
high as the sky
high lonesome

high up to
  picking cotton
higher than a kite
hipped
hit by a barnmouse
hoary-eyed
hocky
hockey
hocus pocus
hog drunk
honked
hooched
hooch up
hoodman
hooted
hopped
hopped-up
hop up
horizontal
hornson
horseback, got the
hosed
hot
hot-headed
hotter than a skunk
how-come-ye-so
illuminated
imbibed too much
in a fix
in a fog
in a fuddle
in a muddle
in a stew
in a trance

in armor
in beer
in color
in drink
in for it
in his airs
in his ales
in his altitudes
in his armor
in his beer
in his glory
in his pots
in his prosperity
in liquor
in orbit
in the bag
in the cellar
in the clouds
in the gutter
in the pen
in the pink
in the pulpit
in the rats
in the sack
in the satchel
in the suds
in the sun
in the tank
in the wind
in uncharted waters
incognito
indisposed
inebriate
inebriated

infirm
influenced
inked
inspired
into the suds
inundated
irrigated
jag up
jagged
jagged-up
jambled
jammed
jarred
jazzed
jazzed-up
Jerusalem, going to
jiggered
jingled
jocular
jolly
jug-bitten
jug-steamed
jugged
juiced
juiced-up
juicy
jungled
kennurd
Kentucky fried
kettle, chase the
kettle, hit his
keyed
keyed-up
keyed to the roof

kib'd heels
kicked in the guts
killed
killed one's dog
king, he's a
king is his cousin
king, seen the French
kisky
kissed the
  Black Betty
kited
knapt
knee-crawling drunk
knee-walking drunk
knocked for a loop
knocked off his pins
knocked out
knocked over
knocked up
knockered
knows the way home
laced
laid out
laid right out
laid to the bone
lame
lap in the gutter
lappy
lathered
leaning
leaping
leaping up
leary
leery

leggs, makes
  indentures with his
legless
leveled
lifted
light
light-headed
likkered
likkered-up
likkerous
limber
limp
lined
lion drunk
liquified
liquor, in
liquor struck
liquor up
liquored
liquored-up
liquorish
listing
lit
lit a bit
lit to the gills
lit to the guards
lit to the gunnels
lit up
lit up like a cathedral
lit up like a
  Christmas tree
lit up like a church
lit up like a
  high mass

lit up like a kite
lit up like
  a skyscraper
lit up like a
  store window
lit up like Broadway
lit up like
  Main Street
lit up like
  Times Square
lit up like the
  Catholic Church
lit up like the sky
little tight
little woozy
live well, to
load one's card
loaded
loaded for bear
loaded his cart
loaded to the barrel
loaded to the
  earlobes
loaded to the gills
loaded to the guards
loaded to the gunnels
loaded to the
  gunwales
loaded to the hat
loaded to the muzzle
loaded to the
  plimsoll mark
lock-legged
logged

look blue about
  the gills
loony
loop-legged
looped
looped-legged
loopy
loose in the hilt
loppy
lord, drunk as a
lordly
lost his rudder
lousy drunk
love-dovey
lubricated
lumped
lumpy
lushed
lushed-up
lushy
mainbrace is
  well-spliced
making scallops
malt is above wheat
  with him
malted
malty
Martin drunk
maudlin
mauled
melted
merry as a grigg
merry pin, on a
methodistconated

middling
milled
mizzled
mocus
moist around
  the edges
monuments,
  raised his
mooney
moon-eyed
mops and brooms
muddled
muddy
mugg blotts
mugged
muggy
mulled
mulled-up
murky
muzzy
nail, off the
nappy
nase
nazie
nazy
nimptopsical
nimtopsical
night mare, got the
nipped
niptopsical
noddy-headed
non compos
noppy
nose is dirty

not all there
not suffering
numb
nuts
nutty
obfuscated
obfusticated
oddish
oenomania
oenophilist
off at the nail
off his bean
off his feet
off the deep end
off to the races
oiled
on his ass
on his ear
on his fourth
on his last legs
on his way out
on the blink
on the floor
on the lee lurch
on the shikker
one-over-eight
one too many
onion, smelt of an
organized
orie-eyed
oscillated
ossified
out
out like a lamp

out like a light
out of his element
out of his mind
out of it
out of one's mind
out of the picture
out of the way
out on the roof
out to lunch
over the bay
over the mark
overboard
overcome
overdone
overloaded
overseas
overseen
overserved
overset
overshot
overtaken
overwined
owl, drunk as an
owl-eyed
owled
oxycrocium
package
package on, have a
packaged
palatic
palled
paralysed
parboiled
past gone

pasted
paunch, wasted his
peckish
pee-eyed
peekish
peonied
pepped
pepst
perked
petrificated
petrified
pickled
pigeon-eyed
pie-eyed
pied
piffed
pifficated
piffled
pigeon-eyed
pilfered
pin drunk
pinked
pinko
pious
piped
pipped
pissed
pixilated
plain drunk
plastered
plated
played out
pleasantly jingled
plonked

plotzed
ploughed
ploughed under
ploxed
pogie
pogy
poggled
pole, up the
polished
polite
polluted
pop-eyed
pot-hardy
pot shaken
pots, among the
pots, in the
pots on
potshot
potsick
potsville
potted
potty
potulent
powder up
powdered
preserved
prestoned
pretty drunk
pretty far gone
pretty happy
pretty high
pretty well plowed
pretty well
  primed priddy

primed to the barrel
primed to the muzzle
primed to the trigger
prosperity, in his
pruned
puggy
punch aboard
pungy
puppy, good-
  conditioned as a
put to bed
  with a shovel
putrid
pye-eyed
quarrelsome
queer
queered
quilted
racked
racked-up
raddled
ragged
raised
rammaged
rampage
rat in trouble
rattled
ratty
raunchy
razzle dazzled
ready
really gassed
really got a load
really lit up

really soused
really tied one on
reeking
reeling
reely
ree-raw
relaxed
religious
rest, at
revved up
rich
rigid
rileyed
ripe
ripped
roasted
rocky
rolling drunk
roostered
rorty
rosined
rosy
rotten
royal rudder, lost his
rum dumb
rummed
rummied
rummed rye
salted
salted down
salubrious
sap happy
sapped
sappy

saturated
sauced
sawed
scammered
schicker
schizzed out
schlitzed
schlockered
schnockered
schnoggered
scoop
scooped
scorched
scrambled
scratched
scraunched
screaming
screaming drunk
screetching
screwed
screwy
scronched
scrooched
scrooped
seafaring
seasick
second hand drunk
seeing a flock
  of moons
seeing bats
seeing bears
seeing double
seeing elephants
seeing the devil

seeing two moons
sell one's senses
sent
served
served-up
set up
sewed
sewed-up
shagged
shagg
shaved
shellacked
shews his hobnails
shick
shicked
shickered
shikker
shikkered
shipwrecked
shitfaced
shitty
shoe pinches him
shorty
shot
shot full of holes
shot in the head
shot in the mouth
shot in the neck
shot in the wrist
shot up
shoulder, burnt his
showing his booze
showing his drinks
showing it

silly
silly drunk
sizzled
skated
skinful
skunk drunk
skunked
skunky
slanted
slathered
sleeve-button
slewed
slewy
slick
slippery
slipping
slobbered
slopped
sloppy
sloshed
sloud
sloughed
slued
slugged
slushed
smashed
smeared
smells of the cork
smitten by the grape
smoked
snackered
snapped snockered
snooted
snootful

snootful, had a
snotted
snozzled
snubbed
snuffy
snug
soaked
soaked his face
soaked to the gills
soaken
soapey-eyed
sobbed
socked
sodden
soft
soggy
sold his senses
Solomon, as wise as
sopped
sopping
soppy
sore-footed
soshed
sotted
sotto
soused
soused to the ears
soused to the gills
southern fried
sow drunk
sozzled
sozzly
sparred
speared

speechless
spiffed
spiffled
spiflicated
splashed
spliced
splifficated
spliffo
sploshed
sponge-eyed
sponge-headed
spotty
spreed
spreeish
sprinkled
sprung
squamed
squared
squashed
squiffed
squiffy
squirrelly
squished
staggerish
staggers
stale drunk
starched
starchy
stark drunk
steady
steamed
steeped
stewed
stewed to the ears

stewed to the gills
sticked
stiff
stiff as a carp
stiff as a goat
stiff as a plank
stiff as a ramrod
stiff as a ring-bolt
stiffed
stimulated
stinkarooed
stinking
stinking drunk
stinko
stitched
stocked up
stoked
stolled
stone blind
stone cold drunk
stoned
stoned out
   of his mind
stonkered
stozzled
striped
stubbed
stuccoed
stung
stunked
stunned
stupefied
stupid
sucked

suds, a little in the
suds, in the
sun, been in the
sun in the eyes
sun over the
   fore-yard
super-charged
swacked
swamped
swatched
swatted
swattled
swazzled
swigged
swiggled
swilled
swilled up
swine drunk
swined
swinnied
swiped
swipy
switched
swiveled
swizzled
swozzled
tacked
tangle-footed
tangled
tangled-legged
tanked
tanked up
tanned
tap-shacklen

taplash wretched
tapped
tapped out
tapped the admiral
tattooed
tean
teeth under
tied one on
tight as a
  ten-day drunk
tilted
tin hats
tinned
tip merry
tin top tippled
Tipiun Grove
tipped
tipping
tippled
tippling
tipsification
tipsified
tipsy
tip-top
tired
toasted
tongue-tied
too far north
top-heavy
top-loaded
toped
topped
toppled
topp

topsy turvy
torn up
torrid-tossed
tosticated
totalled
touched
touched off
toxed
toxicated
trammeled
trance, in a
translated
trashed
tripping drunk
tuben
tumbled down
  the sink
tuned
tuned up
twisted
two sheets
  to the wind
ugly
uncorked
under
under full sail
under full steam
under the table
under the weather
underway
unsober
up a tree
up on blocks
up the pole

up to the gills
upholster
upholstered
uppish
upsed
valient
varnished
vinolence
vulcanized
wall-eyed
wallpapered
wassailed
wassailed out
wassailed up
wasted
water cart, on the
water-logged
water-soaked
watered
waxed
way, out of the
weak-jointed
weary
weaving
well away
well-bottled
well-fixed
well-heeled
well-jointed
well-lathered
well-lit
well-lubricated
well-mulled
well-oiled

well-organized

well-primed

well-soaked

well-sprung

wet

wet-handed

wettish

whacked out

what-nosed

whazooed

whiffled

whipcan

whipped

whipsed

whiskeyfied

whiskey-frisky

whiskey-raddled

whiskey shot

whiskey sodden

whiskied

whistle drunk

whittled

whooshed

whoozy

wilted

wine-potted

wine shits

wined up

winey

wing heavy

winterized

wiped

wiped-out

wired

wise

wobbly

woggled

woofled

wooshed

woozy

wrecked

yaupish

zagged

zapped

zin zagged

zin zan

zippen

zissified

zoned

zonked

zorked

zozzled

Bibliography

Ade, G. *The Old-Time Saloon*. New York: Ray Long and Richard R. Smith, 1931.

Aitken, G. A., ed. *The Tatler*. New York: Hadley and Mathews, 1889.

Asbury, H. *The French Quarter* (1936) Repr. New York: Pocket Books, 1955.

Barrere, A. and C. G. Leland. *A Dictionary of Slang, Jargon and Cant*. London: Ballantyne Press, 1889.

Bartlett, J. R. *Dictionary of Americanisms: A Glossary of Words and Phrases Usually Regarded as Peculiar to the United States*. Boston: Little, Brown, and Co., 1896.

Berry, L. V. and M. Van Den Bark. *The American Thesaurus of Slang*. New York: T. Crowell, 1953.

Bierce, A. *The Devil's Dictionary* (1911). Repr. New York: Durer Books, 1958.

Botkin, B. A. *New York City Folklore*. New York: Random House, 1956.

Brewer's Dictionary of Phrase and Fable, Ivor Evans, ed. New York: Harper and Brothers, 1959.

Brophy, J. and E. Partridge. *Songs and Slang of the British Soldier: 1914-1918*. London: Eric Partridge Ltd., 1930.

Brown, I. *Words on the Level*. London: Bodley Head, 1973.

Brown, J. H. *Early American Beverages*. Rutland, Vermont: C. E. Tuttle, Co., 1966.

Carr, J. *The Second Oldest Profession: An Informal History of Moonshining in America*. Englewood Cliffs, New Jersey: Prentice-Hall, 1972.

Carson, G. *The Social History of Bourbon*. New York: Dodd, Mead and Co., 1963.

Cowie, L. W. *A Dictionary of British Social History*. London: G. Bell and Sons, 1973.

Craigie, W. A. and J. R. Hulbert. *A Dictionary of American English*. Chicago: University of Chicago Press, 1944.

Disraeli, I. *Curiosities of Literature*. London: Frederick Warne and Co., 1881.

D'Urfey, T., ed. *Wit and Mirth: Or Pills to Purge Melancholy*. London: W. Pearson, 1876.

Farmer, J. S. and W. E. Henley. *Slang and Its Analogues*. New York: Arno Press, 1970.

Funk, C. E. *Heavens to Betsy!* New York: Harper and Row, 1955.

Grose, F. *A Classical Dictionary of the Vulgar Tongue*. London: F. Leach, 1788.

Hackwood, F. W. *Inns, Ales, and Drinking Customs of Old England.* London: Bracken Books, 1985.

Hall, B. H. *A Collection of College Words and Customs.* Cambridge, Mass.: John Bartlett, 1856.

Hazlitt, W. C. *Faith and Folklore of the British Isles* (1905). Repr. New York: Benjamin Blom, 1965.

Kunz, G. F. *The Curious Lore of Precious Stones.* New York: Dover, 1971.

Levine, H. L. "The Vocabulary of Drunkenness." *Journal of Studies on Alcohol* 42 (1981): 1038-1051.

Marchant, W. T. *In Praise of Ale or Songs, Ballads, Epigrams, and Anecdotes Relating to Beer, Malt, and Hops with Some Curious Particulars Concerning Ale-wives and Brewers Drinking-clubs and Customs.* London: George Redway, 1888.

Marryat, F. *A Diary in America* (1839). Repr. New York: A. A. Knopf, 1962.

Matthews, C. M. *English Surnames.* London: Weidenfeld and Nicolson, 1966.

Maurer, D. W. "The Argot of the Moonshiner," *American Speech* 24 (1949).

Mencken, H. L. *The American Language.* Supplement 1. New York: A. A. Knopf, 1945, 200.

Mencken, H. L. *The American Language.* New York: A. A. Knopf, 1936.

Morris, W. and M. Morris. *Dictionary of Word and Phrase Origins.* New York: Harper and Row, 1977.

Nares. R. *A Glossary;* or, *Collection of Words, Phrases, Names, and Allusions to Customs, Proverbs, etc., Which Have Been Thought to Require Illustration in the Works of English Authors, Particularly Shakespeare and His Contemporaries.* Revised by J. O. Halliwell and T. Wright. London: Reeves and Turner, 1888.

Oxford English Dictionary. New York: Oxford University Press, 1973.

Palmer, A. S. *Folk-Etymology* (1883). Repr. New York: Greenwood Press, 1969.

Partridge, E. *A Dictionary of Slang and Unconventional English.* New York: Macmillan Pub. Co., 1974.

Reaney, P. H. *The Origin of English Surnames.* New York: Barnes and Noble, 1967.

Reany, P. H. and R. M. Wilson. *A Dictionary of British Surnames.* London: Routledge and Kegan Paul, 1977.

Revel, J. F. *Culture and Cuisine: A Journey Through the History of Food.* Garden City, N.Y.: Doubleday & Co., 1982.

Shay, F. *A Sailor's Treasury.* New York: W. W. Norton, 1951.

Thornton, R. H. *An American Glossary.* Philadelphia: J. B. Lippincott, 1912.

Ware, J. R. *Passing English of the Victorian Era* (1909) Repr. New York: EP Publishing Ltd., 1972.

Weekley, E. *Words Ancient and Modern.* London: John Murray, 1946.

Weseen, M. H. *A Dictionary of American Slang.* New York: Thomas Y. Crowell Co., 1934.